To Mary,

with affection and sincere gratitude for a caring and greatly valued friendship. I hope the reading will revive happy memories.

Sincerely,

David

A DRAGON IN THE HOUSE

A Dragon in the House

DAVID ROSSER

Gomer Press

First Impression—September 1987

© David Rosser

ISBN 0 86383 357 8

Printed in Wales by
J. D. Lewis & Sons Ltd., Gomer Press, Llandysul, Dyfed

To Myfanwy, whose encouragement, tolerance, support and loving understanding has made it all possible.

CONTENTS

Page

Foreword ix

Introduction x

Chapter

1 The End—and a Beginning 1

2 The Die is Cast 4

3 Those First Steps 10

4 The Lobby 18

5 How it all began 34

6 Smoke-room Secrets 39

7 Eat, Drink and be merry 44

8 Breach of Privilege 48

9 A Voice for Wales 60

10 Welsh Voices 78

11 On and off the Air 88

12 Cardiff and the Welsh Development Corporation 94

13 Dai Grenfell 99

14 Iron and Steel 105

15 Some Famous Stories and Characters 121

16 Prime Ministers I have known 150

17 Neil Kinnock . . . Still Future Prime Minister? 189

18 Two Tragedies 198

19 Mr Speaker Thomas 208

20 The Speaker speaks 218

21 Decline and Fall 227

FOREWORD

David Rosser joined the Lobby of the House of Commons as representative of the *Western Mail* in my first year as an M.P.. Throughout my career in the Commons he was my close friend and confidant.

I was always aware that he always had close ties with Cabinet Ministers whichever Party was in office. He became one of the best-informed Lobby correspondents in Parliament and his shrewd assessments, both of issues and of parliamentarians, never failed to impress me.

Like his colleagues in the Press Lobby, he probably carried far more Parliamentary secrets than he was ever able to publish. The total trust which exists between experienced members of the Press Lobby and M.P.'s is an essential part of the machinery of Parliament. It ensures that Press correspondents are able to write responsible and shrewd comments on happenings in Westminster. Long experience in the Press Lobby also enables journalists to develop a sixth sense for guessing when political activity is under way.

After almost four decades' service in the House of Commons and House of Lords Press Lobby, David Rosser's memoirs cover twelve Parliaments. He has dealt personally with every leading politician in the U.K. since the last war. His memoirs will serve to fill in the gaps left in the memoirs of we politicians, and also to enable people to interpret Parliamentary activities and manoeuvres with greater understanding.

I am glad that David Rosser has decided to let us see Parliament through the discerning eyes of a journalist whose affection for the Mother of Parliaments is second to none.

George Thomas—Tonypandy

INTRODUCTION

It is five years since I retired as Political Editor of the *Western Mail*. It had been "my paper" ever since I accepted the offer to leave the weekly and evening paper scenes to become the *Mail*'s man in Port Talbot way back in 1938. Thanks to the generosity of the present management of the paper I have no immediate inclination to remove myself from Westminster, which has been my life for the past four decades. With the benign consent of the Editor and the goodwill of the authorities of the House (and with divine approval, of course) I may be fortunate enough to be still treading the well-worn paths from the Gallery to the Lobbies and through the corridors and to be able to mingle with colleagues and Members well into 1989.

Now that would be something! But I do not intend to put it to the test before I share with others the experiences which have already been my lot at the centre of the political force which affects us all. I have been pressurised from many quarters to record those events in which I have been personally involved or been party to in the immediate post-war years at Westminster, and subsequently. There have been quite a number worth recording, I assure you. And as I relive, in my mind and on paper, those historic years and events, I have come to recognise how extremely fortunate I am to have been so often at the very heart of events which have figured in the evolution (or devolution, depending on personal preferences) from the British Empire to the Commonwealth, and experienced at first hand, and often contributed to, the marked changes in the standards of political, economic, social and other aspects of our daily existence. And by no means least of those changes—and one which has been the biggest general effect—has been in public morality.

In many areas comparisons are acceptable, but critical judgments cannot but be subject to scepticism where there are vested political, moral or ethnic interests. Which is why I do not subject my views of the changes to any single political outlook. By virtue of the system which has prevailed for more than a century, and during which has grown up a special relationship between us as Lobby Correspondents and those with whom we are in daily contact in pursuit of our work and responsibilities, it would be not only difficult but unwise and unfair to ally oneself openly to one party or political ideology.

To do so would court problems of association, and a good Lobby Correspondent is acceptable as much to those of the right or centre as to those of the left and either extreme. The changes of standards over the years I have spent at Westminster must be attributed in various measures to the policies and ideological thinking of successive governments of whatever political shade. These include the Utopian ideal of equality in all things as between the sexes and in all material issues, the opposing concepts of privatisation and nationalisation, the conflicts over nuclear and conventional defence systems, the almost total failure to come up with a reasonable antidote to mass unemployment, and also the inevitability of facing up to the provision of leisure pursuits for the masses as the labour force gets smaller. There is a hard core among M.P.'s who regard the latter as the most important and also the most difficult problem facing future governments.

Soon there will be an overwhelming need for non-occupational therapies for the increasing numbers of the retired and the redundant. Capping it all will be the problem of how to finance and sustain these new political and social challenges of the future. To this background I am becoming increasingly more conscious of a deep longing for the restoration of those qualities of everyday life which, for many and varied reasons, have disappeared or been rejected, to be replaced by an apparent national despair. We are in danger of accepting as a general norm of existence daily accounts of hooliganism and thuggery, a degeneration of moral, social and even religious standards, and a bitter hopelessness which is increasingly pervading the ranks of average school-leavers and maturing adults. There is a growing tendency to succumb to the lure of severance pay, and the Golden Handshake has become the accepted alternative to a normal retirement.

These problems are recognised by our political leaders. They are argued about in committees, of which there is a plethora at Westminster, responsible for the ground-work on respective party policies. But, as is ever the case in politics, considerations are governed by vote-catching. It must be hoped that some day, and soon, authority will cast aside the dominant factor of the political scene, which has been to win the biggest share of votes, and face up to the real facts. The Nation is slumping into a virulent malaise and the cause is not only unemployment and an unstable economy. Indiscipline and ceasing to care for anything and anyone are root causes which must be tackled ruthlessly to get the Nation back on to the right track.

Chapter 1: The End—and a Beginning

"Who Goes Home?" . . . Eerily the call went echoing through the corridors of the Palace of Westminster. Tonight, for the first time, I found it depressing—yet I must have heard it thousands of times before, and never had it affected me in this way.

It had been a heavy day again. The Commons had sat on until near midnight. The M.P. for Bolsover and a few supporting colleagues had concluded the Adjournment Debate, the final business of every day.

The Clerks at the Table announced the end of this day's deliberations. The Keeper of the Door to the Members' Lobby nodded to the senior Lobby police officer and the cry went out, to be taken up by other officers at strategic points throughout the labyrinth of the Palace. "Who Goes Home?" has been the time-honoured signal and summons to all M.P.'s at the end of a working-day since way back, when Westminster, seat of the first democratic government, had been surrounded by open land and foot-pads preyed on lonely pedestrians late at night. So M.P.'s were gathered into bands to be escorted to their homes in the City.

I had heard it so often and tonight it struck me to the heart. Tomorrow, for the first time in four decades, I should be absent from the familiar scene. This was my final day as Lobby Correspondent and the severance was weighing heavily upon me.

Of course there *would* be occasions when I should come back for visits and re-stoke the memories of reporting triumphs and disappointments. But it would never be the same. *Tonight* I was an accredited member of one of the great Parliamentary institutions, the Lobby Journalists. *Tomorrow* I should be an ex-member, shorn of all the privileges and standing which being a member—the senior in service—of that august body offered.

Alone at my desk, a favoured vantage-point which looked over New Palace Yard, Parliament Square, and beyond to the towering spires and graceful arches of Westminster Abbey, I suddenly realised the pangs I was suffering, a tearing at the soul, a mental anguish.

The rules of employment decreed that at 65 I must retire. But why *should* I give it all up? I was mentally and physically fit. I had acquired a wealth of experience and that feel for political developments which comes from personal, instructive contacts with the nation's administrators. Suddenly, with a bitterness such as I had never experienced before, I didn't want to go!

In the months preceding my departure I had built up a pleasant picture of retirement. My wife and I would be able to enjoy many things we had so often talked about and which, owing to the exigencies of the service which frequently kept me at the House until the early hours of the morning, had almost always been out of our reach. For more than twenty-five years we had savoured the pleasures of caravanning only during the long summer Parliamentary Recess. In retirement there would be no unsocial hours to restrict our movements, no government crises or Cabinet changes (usually at weekends) to tie me down. Great! We should be free to roam at will: Utopia was within our reach.

Yet, staring out of the window which had been my unobscured view of so many great State occasions over the years, and with the midnight chimes of Big Ben—it was less than thirty yards away—still reverberating through my room, Room 10 in the Upper Corridor of the Parliamentary Press Gallery, I felt that my world had come to an end. Dramatic it might seem—but how many people have experienced, from the *inside*, the events which fashion world-decisions or seen, as I had seen, the reduction of an Empire to a limited Colonial administration, thence to a Commonwealth of former British territories, and, finally, the merger, for economic reasons, into the European Community? And how many, apart from elected Members and

Peers of the Realm or Officers of the House, have enjoyed membership of the Most Exclusive Club in the World?

Was it the loss of my privileges that was casting me into such gloom? Partly, I suppose. But mainly it was the realisation that I should no longer be a player on the great Westminster Stage; no longer be able to record, and participate in the running of Parliament.

There had been no farewell celebrations—a break with custom, since long-serving colleagues were expected to provide the "free pint" at the Press Bar to temper a sad occasion, a kind of Parliamentary Wake. I had been left alone with my thoughts, in a rebellious frame of mind at the prospect that, once I had walked through the door, across the cobbled New Palace Yard into Whitehall and entered my car parked in Horse Guards Parade, it was the end of an era.

During this, my final half hour as an accredited representative—Lobby Correspondent and Political Editor of the *Western Mail*, which I had served in and out of Westminster for forty-three years—I found images of the past coming powerfully to mind. That terrible night of storm and shipwreck at Sker Point which, in effect, began it all; my solitary, but less than stately, drive along the Royal Route; how Guy Eden saved my career; who drank Winnie's Nectar; Hugh Dalton, incapably drunk; Gwynfor Evans refusing the Oath of Allegiance; how Labour gagged my broadcasts; Dai Grenfell in tears—and in virile pursuit; the forging and failing of iron and steel; Nye Bevan, at Brighton in 1957, aimlessly knocking snooker-balls around the table before his hardest decision; Von Rundstedt; nine Prime Ministers and a potential tenth; the tragedies of Desmond Donnelly and Lady Megan Lloyd George; Mr Speaker Thomas, a friend for life; the C.B.E. lost and the M.B.E. won. Experiences and situations, surely, to be treasured and shared.

Chapter 2: The Die is Cast

How was it that someone with only the slightest political interest, and practically no knowledge of party politics except what was carried in the newspapers, came to be appointed Politicial Correspondent for the *Western Mail*, a newspaper held in the highest esteem in regard of its political content (if not its then right-wing views)?

The first approach came when my Editor, David Prosser, asked whether I was interested in a specialist job. The position as the paper's Political Correspondent was being canvassed among the staff in line with the commitment that it would be open to those returning from active service. It had, I understood, been made known to the present occupier, Sylvan Howells, that his appointment was a wartime one and in that sense only temporary.

Frankly, I was scared at the prospect. I was a district correspondent for Bridgend and the very large area embracing the Vale of Glamorgan and the Garw and Ogmore valleys as far west as Port Talbot. It was the largest reporting area of the paper and after six and a half years of active service I relished my return to these wide open spaces and to being virtually my own boss again. Besides, it was the area I had been in charge of before the war, when it had offered the widest scope in general reporting.

At that time the thought of London did not appeal to me, but in February 1947 I was called to Cardiff and told the job lay between me and Alan Jones, the Rhondda correspondent, a very experienced and reliable journalist who was older than I. The difference in our age made him, in my eyes, the favourite for the post, but the appointment and its confirmation was still some four months away. The turning-point, in fact, was to come two months after that interview.

On the evening of April 23rd the Liberty Ship, S.S. Samtampa, making its way up the Bristol Channel towards Newport in the teeth of a growing storm, broke down. Without

Sker Point Tragedy, 1947: Wreck of the Mumbles Lifeboat.

power, it drifted towards the notorious Sker Point Rocks, Porthcawl, where it was wrecked with the loss of forty seamen, its entire crew. Shortly after midnight the Mumbles lifeboat went missing and was also wrecked. Its entire crew of eight perished in the attempted rescue.

It was the worst ever maritime disaster on the Welsh coastline, costing forty-eight lives, and it happened in my area. Again, I suppose, it was my good fortune that I happened to be in the right place at the right time because within half an hour of the ship being driven onto the rocks, and thanks to a tip-off from a friendly Porthcawl police officer, I had joined a small band of Coastguards on the sand dunes only three hundred yards from where the stricken vessel was being pounded and ripped into pieces. It was terrible, but we were utterly helpless in the teeth of a howling gale, with sixty foot waves lashing the Sker Rocks and seeming to sharpen each jagged fang to an even finer point of destruction. Nothing that anyone or anything could do, it seemed, could bring succour to the hapless crew. I was a constant witness to the disaster, which became a ten-hour nightmare.

The full story has been printed several times, and I won the Kemsley National Journalist of the Year commendation for the running eyewitness account I was able to telephone direct to the newsroom on an open line from Sker Farm, which virtually overlooked the scene. The story was being continuously updated for each edition of the paper until 3.30 a.m.

Then, the final episode of a ten-hour vigil. With dawn breaking and the storm fully abated, and with searchers ferreting around the oil-strewn rocks in a heartbreaking search for victims, Police Sergeant Austin and I left the farm and clambered down to the sandy foreshore. We trudged along the beach and, rounding a dune, came across yellow oilskin-covered bodies. They were the crewmen of the fourteen-ton Mumbles lifeboat, "Edward, Prince of Wales".

Just a hundred yards further on was the upturned boat itself, with a gaping hole in its side where the razor-sharp rocks had ripped it asunder.

Within minutes I was back on the telephone and the duty sub-editor, at my pleading, ordered a re-plate of the front page. The *Western Mail* had the exclusive story. It won me the award and a presentation from Lord Kemsley, but more than that, it clinched my appointment as Lobby Correspondent. Confirmation was given to me personally at the scene of the disaster by my Editor, who along with the London Editor, Mr. Edward James, a native of Porthcawl, had motored down to see the wreck.

Two months later I was at Westminster to begin a new career which would span nearly forty years, and which resulted in my becoming the first Political Editor of the *Western Mail*. For that appointment I had to thank David Thomas, the Managing Editor, and Duncan Gardiner, the then Editor, and also the support and acknowledgement which the proposal received from my former Editor, David Cole, then Managing Director of

Thomson Regional Newspapers, of which the *Western Mail* was one.

My first days in the Lobby were very lonely ones. I had been told to ask for Sylvan Howells, who would introduce me to my new colleagues in the Lobby and show me the ropes. But Mr. Howells was nowhere to be found. Westminster seemed a vast, uncaring place for a newcomer, full of people hurrying about their own business. Some policemen, however, (many of whom later became close personal friends) enquired if they could be of assistance. What a far call from the strict security procedures of today when, at the least suspicion of being "strangers without genuine business", the public are challenged—should they have been able, in the first place, to gain admission through any of the many entrances to the building. To solicitous police enquiries I found that my reply, "I'm a Lobby Correspondent," gave me the entrée to almost any part of the Palace.

Sylvan's absence was explained to me by Douglas Haig, then Lobby Correspondent for the *Liverpool Post*. He was in the throes of moving back to Wales (Cardiganshire) and had left the message for me to carry on. He would be returning in a few days and be with me in the following week. My first week at Westminster, therefore, I spent alone, acquainting myself with the order of things, finding out what being in the Lobby meant and introducing myself to Welsh M.P.'s. My primary consideration, I had been told by Mr. James, was Welsh M.P.'s and Welsh affairs. National politics would be looked after by the Press Association and other agencies.

I firmly believe that having to go it alone in that first week did more for my confidence and personal relationships with M.P.'s than anything else could have done.

Bearing in mind I had never set foot in the Palace, and that I had been plunged into a mighty vortex of power with hardly any instruction, that week left an indelible mark. I discovered that, despite all the visible currents of vicious party-political strife,

there was an underlying spirit of camaraderie between M.P.'s
and the Press Gallery and Lobby which removed a lot of the
toughness and stress of tenure at Westminster. There was a
kind of family feeling. Whereas today "The Press" arouses
general hostility, M.P.'s did not then regard the presence of
parliamentary journalists as an intrusion into their personal or
party-political pursuits.

One of the foremost requirements of a successful Lobby Correspondent is to have the luck to be in the right place at the right
time. I was lucky enough in my first week to come across a
story which, although not of any party or political importance,
nonetheless gave me my first experience of the "power of the
Press".

Roderic Bowen, Q.C., M.P. (centre).

The first M.P. with whom I made contact was Roderic Bowen, K.C., then Liberal M.P. for Cardigan and an old acquaintance from my police court reporting days at Bridgend. Having exchanged formalities and been given a welcome to the House, I was asked by him to call attention to the poor state of the facilities on the overnight train service between Paddington and Fishguard. Bowen used this service frequently, sometimes two or three times a week. Sleeping bunks *were* available, but passengers had only brown paper towels for their ablutions before disembarking.

"See if you can get Paddington to do something about this," Mr. Bowen urged. Wartime travelling conditions were still very much in evidence then, even though we were into 1947. He gave me a few quotes and suggested a London Letter paragraph in the *Western Mail* might have some effect. It could also lead to a question in the House! Here, then, was my first parliamentary story:

"Let there be a return to the more civilised cotton towels on sleeper trains where there is a growing demand."

It led to a vigorous exchange of letters, with Paddington the butt. Shortly afterwards the Western Region brought back "proper towels" . . . mostly from large *pre-war* stocks, I heard . . . and my first campaigning effort had been rewarded.

Not only did this do a lot for my ego, but it laid a sound base for association and communication with backbench M.P.'s. It was on that basis that I built a firm and mutually beneficial relationship with "my M.P.'s" throughout my duration at Westminster.

Chapter 3: Those First Steps

After four decades in the Lobbies of the House of Commons and the House of Lords, and at the heart of the political scene with its evolving ethos and pathos, the time has come to put on record events which have contributed, in measures large and small, to the post-war changes within Britain: the end of an Empire and the development of the Commonwealth. I have been close to them all, an unbiased but involved witness.

My involvement was primarily with Wales and with Welsh affairs, but inevitably a larger slice was concerned with events and issues far beyond the Principality. Mine could well prove to be the longest period of personal service in the British Lobby for any Lobby Correspondent. Certainly it has been one packed with history and intimate associations with the elected Members and Peers of the Mother of Parliaments, and a lifetime incorporating at least twelve governments and nine Prime Ministers, not to mention more than fifty Budgets (including the Dennis Healey minis).

Within this span have been shared confidences covering the whole spectrum of political life and a personal association with events which have left their mark on Britain and the British way of life. From Prime Ministers to the newest backbenchers, and throughout the entire hierarchy of government officials and departmental staffs, secrets and confidences of many kinds have been shared and sustained. By the very nature of the Lobby Correspondent's code of ethics—and none is stricter in any aspect of public life—many confidences must remain such where they involve those, in and out of Parliament and political life, who are still with us. But there are a great many others which can and will be told. Where I consider I am no longer bound to the Lobby undertaking, these will now be shared, and there is a lot to be revealed.

The outward face of Westminster has changed over the past forty years, as much as have its occupants, its modes and its general atmosphere. The cobbled yard has been replaced largely by an elegant landscaped walk, the centrepiece of which is the Tudor Fountain erected on the very site of Henry VIII's favourite fountain discovered when New Palace Yard was being disembowelled to provide underground car parks for the M.P.'s. A strange thing is that the walks are seldom used by M.P.'s and their guests nowadays but, looking down from my workroom desk in Room 10/5, three windows removed from Big Ben's tower, I always found the area a fascinating link with the Tudor period.

My first encounter with Westminster Hall, with a thousand years of history permeating its lofty, roof-bearing hammer beams, and its vastness exaggerated by the absence of a single roof-bearing column, gave me an eerie feeling, the more so because it was almost deserted at the time. That could not happen today when, in and out of working days, thousands pound the stone-flagged floor where brass plates mark the spots of great historical happenings.

I remember climbing slowly the historic steps which had been mounted by King Charles I to learn the verdict of execution by the axe, and by so many other famous people in history. I moved into St. Stephen's Hall, where Wat Tyler summoned the first Parliament at Westminster and where four brass studs mark the position of the first "Speaker's" chair. I recall being very conscious of stepping into history. I should have been nervous of what lay before me, but I wasn't. Instead, I felt for the first time that I was facing a great challenge and a new life and I determined there and then that I would make a success of it.

When I moved into the Central Lobby, which later I discovered was the meeting place and connecting link between elected representatives and their constituents, I felt disappointed. It was under repair from the ravages of German bombs which, in 1940, had destroyed the Chamber of the House of Commons but fortunately had not caused much damage to other parts of the Palace. What struck me most then was the row of telephone kiosks halfway around the circular Lobby, blocking off the entrance to the old Chamber. I later found they were for the use of M.P.'s who, at that time, had no offices or telephones available and who did much of their secretarial work in them.

Compared with those days our present M.P.'s are cossetted beyond measure. For their predecessors the task of replying to the daily post-bag more often than not meant letters written by hand and without the aid of secretaries or researchists. Those who did have these aids had to pay for them themselves. In fairness, however, the M.P.'s post-bag then was nothing in comparison with today's.

Another thing which struck me at the time was the emptiness of the Central Lobby. It is very different today. Not once was I stopped or challenged by any of the special and trusted House of Commons and Lords police force. How vastly different now!

Little did I realise then that I would traverse that route many thousands of times before my daily attendance at the House would come to an end. Little, too, did I realise that before my time there would be up, Westminster would be transformed into a security cocoon where no one enters without being checked and challenged, and where security forces have, of necessity, had to be increased tenfold. As with the community and rural policing of yesteryear those early post-war days at Westminster enjoyed a Members-to-police relationship very similar to that between the Bobby on the beat and his public.

The Commons-Lords police were a handpicked group who came under the control of nearby Cannon Row police station and Old Scotland Yard. They knew by sight those Peers and M.P.'s in daily attendance at the Palace. There was a close, friendly and trusting relationship and the wheels turned smoothly, with a minimum of officiousness.

Those on the various point-duties were known by their christian names and were always helpful and kindly disposed to a closely-knit House of Commons. It seems now as though I am referring to another era and another place, and I suppose that, judged by present day practice, I am. On reflection, this is what has given rise lately to a yearning for the "good old days". The changes around us have been multiple, most of them forced upon us and not of choice. It has had to be acceptable among those who, like myself, look back with great nostalgia to the better times, that present conditions are a reflection of the general malady which has afflicted our country, and which is lamentably and perniciously eroding the proud prefix from "Great Britain" throughout the world.

My introduction to the Parliamentary scene, possible the biggest adventure of my life, remains as vivid today as on my thirty-second birthday, 16th June 1947. Despite six and a half years' service with the Royal Air Force, I was still an overawed lad from the sticks when I reported to Fleet Street for my first official meeting with Mr. Edward James, London Editor of the *Western Mail*, one time Lobby Correspondent and, without doubt, one of the great figures of the Street.

In those days the *Western Mail* and the *South Wales Echo*, its sister paper in Cardiff, shared a single-fronted office at the top of Fleet Street, next to Peel's, the famous public house greatly favoured by journalists, printers, and lawyers from nearby Temple Chambers. The office was, without question, a focal point of London Welsh life and interests, and closely connected with the London Welsh Club of Grays Inn Road.

The editorial office of two rooms on the first of the three-floor building was the unquestioned domain of Eddie James and his staff: Charles Pugh (who was more adept at covering short stories and gathering facts and gossip about Welsh affairs in London than anyone I knew), and Gwilym Davies, who had surrendered his active reporting talents to become Mr. James's "composing secretary", a mere shorthand copyist. Eddie James rarely wrote his stories, and especially his scintillating and famous daily London Letter, and the weekend column "Talk in the Clubs'' feature. He preferred to dictate to Gwilym whilst himself noting in shorthand, on any ready-to-hand pieces of paper, a check-note.

On this particular day, 16th June 1947, I had turned up early to await the great man's arrival. I suppose I thought I would be given a formal introduction and a lecture on what would be expected of me as the new *Western Mail* Lobby Correspondent, a post previously held, since the early 1900's, by only four staff men. These were Sir Emsley Carr (who later became the *News of the World* baron), then Mr Edward James, who was joined by Mr. Idris Thomas, and a wartime appointment to replace Mr. Thomas, who returned to Cardiff as Assistant Editor of the *Western Mail*. This was Mr Sylvan Howell.

I was to take over from Mr. Howell a job in which I had only the slightest conception of what was required of me; hence my expectation of a formal guidance by Mr. James. The interview went something like this:

"Well, have you had a look around . . . do you know London?"

Did I know London? I had been to the Big City only a few times, one of which was a couple of years before the war when I had come to Fleet Street to apply for a reporting job on the old *Daily Sketch*,—so I answered truthfully, "Very little, sir, but I came here by car."

"Do you know your way to the House of Commons by car?"

"Afraid not, Mr. James."

"Where's your car now?"

"Outside the office." It had been there for about an hour already. (What a sign of changed times! Just try and leave an unattended car in Fleet Street today, even for a few minutes!)

I learned a great deal from Eddie James during our twenty-six years' association, but nothing was more important, nor more fundamental to my new career, than the advice he gave me then.

"Right," he said brusquely. "Drive down the Strand to Traf-

algar Square and as you turn into Whitehall and past the Cenotaph you will see Big Ben and the high railings of Westminster
on your left. When you come to the first big iron gates you drive
straight in.'' Now came the important lesson. ''A policeman
will try to stop you, but you drive past, just as if you were an
M.P. Be sure of yourself and I'll be surprised if you are challenged again.''

That ''be sure of yourself'' in such a situation was a tip worth
its weight in gold. I followed it assiduously thereafter and it
rarely let me down.

As I swept though the tall gates, with a pounding heart but
showing a friendly smile to the policeman, I hardly realised I
was entering an entirely new career in journalism which was to
span the administrations of nine Prime Ministers and which
was to make me the friend and confidant of a great many political and parliamentary figures both at home and abroad.

A sequel a few days later also taught me a valuable lesson.
With an increasing boldness I had been repeating the manoeuvre through the entrance gate. A confidant nod to the officer
on point and an elegant sweep through into the cobbled yard
had proved sufficient. Then I noticed the officer I had passed on
my first day bearing down on me. As I got out of the car he
approached casually and asked if he could look it over. Not a
word about me. The car was the object of attraction.

I loved that car, a pre-war Triumph Gloria, bright green and
with a fold-back hood. It dazzled the eye with a mass of spark-
ling chromium-plated lattice work in front of the radiator and
two headlamps which closely resembled twin searchlights.
That was in the days when most vehicles on the roads were still
drab. It wasn't me or my grand entrance a few days earlier that
had aroused the policeman's curiosity. It taught me that, thereafter, if I was to carry through successfully the Eddie James
maxim, it would have to be with a low profile, and not by
calling attention to oneself. I have always remembered it, and it
has paid its dividends many more times than I can calculate.

On another occasion this car nearly brought me into conflict with the authorities. It happened during a Royal Opening of Parliament.

On such occasions the processional route from Constitution Hill, alongside Buckingham Palace to the Palace of Westminster is always closed to public traffic from about an hour before the Sovereign's Escort moves out of the Buckingham forecourt.

In those days there were no passes, and no badges for those of us who used the House of Commons car parking space in New Palace Yard. Press Gallery members and Lobby journalists had their gallery cards of accreditation, and M.P.'s faces were *their* identifications. So when I arrived very late at the top of Constitution Hill to find entry barred, I flashed my Gallery pass and shouted to the police, "House of Commons, very urgent!" Before I knew it, I was driving fast down the route, which was flanked by the Guards.

It was my intention to get out of this embarrassing situation by driving down The Mall into Trafalgar Square. But the road was blocked by an unbroken line of Guards. I looked desperately for an opening to dodge out. There was none. I was forced to keep going, cheered on by the crowds which packed the route. The Triumph, resplendent in its bright green colour and flashing chromium plate, must have been the only moving object along the Royal route and this was sufficient to bring loud and sporadic cheers from the crowds. It was ludicrous.

I was hot and cold all over as I swung into Horse Guards Parade, still flanked by the Guards and cheering crowds (possibly they thought I was the vanguard of the Royal Coach!) As I swung into Whitehall through the St. James Arch and around the King Charles statue, the road ahead was clear, but I could not turn right or left. There was still that unbroken line of soldiers and the still cheering crowds. This was awful. I was trapped. The Houses of Parliament were not more than five hundred yards away and still I was driving on. I had visions of having to drive right up to Chancellor's Gate at the House of

Lords where the Sovereign descends, with all the horrible repercussions that would bring.

Suddenly, out of the corner of my eye, I spotted a movement. There was a break in the line of Guards right at the gated entrance to New Palace Yard and without any warning I turned in sharply. As with Moses and the Red Sea, the opening closed abruptly behind me. I was safe. And nobody came up to me to say a single word. It had been a terrifying experience and I must have aged twenty years in that five minutes' drive. I often wondered afterwards what those cheering crowds and the marshalls must have thought was happening as that solitary vehicle and its desperate driver came cruising down the route.

Chapter 4: The Lobby

When I joined it the Lobby was a much different body to that of today. There were no more than a score of us in daily attendance, representing almost every newspaper throughout the world either directly or through agencies—the Press Association, Exchange Telegraph, and Reuters. It was, too, in a sense a much more casual life, especially on the output side.

It was quality much more than quantity which mattered in those early days. By that I mean one was not expected to file two, three, four or more "inside" political stories a day. Today a Lobby Correspondent is not thought to be on top of the job unless he or she (and that is another big change in the Lobby's composition, since no one ever contemplated then anything other than a male Lobby Correspondent) turns in numerous pieces every day and regularly makes the front page.

The male bastion has long been breached. Over the past ten years women correspondents have lined up alongside their male colleagues with distinction. In 1986, for the first time in its century of tradition, the Lobby even chose its first female Chairman. In the same year the Press Gallery elected its first female Vice-Chairman, so 1986 must go on record as the year of the great break-through.

Another change has been that "The Lobby" has become an institution known and recognised outside Westminster and Parliamentary circles and activities. Numerically it has grown and grown—the Little Topsy of Parliament—until today its membership has topped the 150 mark. Its make-up now includes the so-called Corps D'élite of television and radio (with the BBC and Independent TV and radio teams, together with their administrative echelons, greatly outnumbering all others) and the National dailies' and Sunday newspapers' numbers one, two, and alternates.

As the Lobby has grown in numbers so it has in activities, although regrettably its strength and influence have not kept pace. The reason is fairly simple. During the immediate pre-war and post-war days the output of legislation at Westminster was on a much reduced scale, and governments were allowed more rein and less interference from the Floor of the House of Commons in getting on with the job of governing; so there were fewer inside-stories to relate or reveal. The events at Westminster were largely confined to activities on the floor of the House and the debates were dutifully reported by the Press Gallery.

The Lobby Correspondent's purpose was to keep an eye on inside operations, to bring to the electorate and the general public the reason for, and explanation of, Bills as they appeared, and to keep abreast of government and various party-political policies as they affected the people.

Cabinets, as the heart and soul of all governments, are of particular interest to the Lobby, and on the tried and tested basis of the Lobby's ethics of confidentiality it was not surprising that much information was fed to Correspondents.

There was always a close understanding between authoritative informants and their Lobby Correspondents in those days. Once having been given the promise of confidence, Ministers and M.P.'s, alike could be sure that the recipient would not rush into print before the confidence had been released. To give or receive information "on Lobby terms" was a gilt-edged understanding. It was the Code of the Lobby, one which was not lightly regarded. Once proved guilty of a breach of confidence, an accused Lobby Correspondent might just as well pack up and, in the interest of his paper and its accreditation, leave the Lobby for other fields. There have, however, been remarkably few cases where this has happened.

Markedly changed as the Lobby is today, with its top-heavy membership and constant and highly competitive operations which make the achievement of a "scoop" virtually a thing of the past, there is none-the-less still a very strict observation of that code of ethics on confidences—except that, where there are so many participants in a story, confidences are increasingly difficult to sustain.

Whilst the principle, if not the system, is as strong today as it was at its inception more than a century ago, it cannot but be admitted by its members that the Lobby has suffered a serious setback in its image in recent years. ''Leaks'' which have been attributed to individuals, but which cast a critical reflection upon the Lobby as a whole, have repeatedly soured relationships with No. 10 Downing Street, the Lobby's main channel to government sources of information, several government departments, and particularly with Parliamentary committees and rank-and-file Members.

Unless these can be repaired and the Lobby, as a corporate body of first-class journalists, operating within the extensive confines of Westminster on such exceptional privileges, regains the universal respect which has always been synonymous with its title, its existence could well be in jeopardy. Difficult it undoubtedly will be, whilst the Lobby grows in numbers, to sustain the level of confidence which has been its hallmark, but its history is such that its elected officers will surely find a way to re-establish its authority and essential place within the political and parliamentary scenes.

There are ways of employing confidences without entirely losing out on news and commentary services. But to reveal in print chunks of important and controversial reports, many of them ''privileged'' before the time of publication, just to gain a short-term advantage at the expense of colleagues and the Lobby as a body, or to treat a confidence in such a way as to point to its source, is so completely out of character that there can be no justification for it. The Lobby has lost face among many of Parliament's 650 M.P.'s, and also the newer breed of Life Peers who now, more than at any time in our history, are involved in all the processes of legislation. It has to search its own soul to sustain a tradition which established a hard-won niche at Westminster in the past hundred years of its parliamentary and political history.

Parliament has developed over the past thirty years into a legislative sausage-machine which is making it more and more difficult for the Lobby Correspondent singly to cope with. Another chore which has to be carried out now, and almost daily, are the countless committees. In addition to the Standing Committees to which Bills are referred off the Floor of the House are the Select Committees, the Grand Committees, the various political party committees, and official and unofficial back-bench committees. It has become the practice over recent years to keep an eye on them all. Officials involved with the lesser non-parliamentary committees see to it that Lobby Correspondents are kept primed with any controversial aspects. Over the years they have become aware of the tremendous public relations advantages of bringing in the Lobby journalists. The result has been a vast increase in the work-load, and the quantity has frequently impaired the quality of Lobby output.

In keeping with Parliament, the Lobby itself has become a constantly tapped information machine. I often wonder, in the retrospection of the past forty years, where is it going to end?

When there were so few in the Lobby, a mere handful of accredited correspondents for the National Dailies, the three London evening newspapers and BBC radio, together with some of the bigger and longer-established regional newspapers (and that is how it was until 1952, when evening newspapers generally were first admitted) there was an aura of mystique about it and its operations. I felt as if I had been admitted to the Magic Circle.

First and foremost there was the strict Code of Confidence which has been the basic tenet of Lobby journalists, and without which there could be no co-existence with the Members of the House of Commons and their Lordships in what is termed "The Other Place". To commit a breach of confidence by revealing what one had been told "on Lobby terms" was, I was told, to let down the whole institution.

Of course, it was explained to me, there was no bounden reason why one should operate only on the basis of confidence so long as one's informant was told from the beginning that a confidence on any particular matter was not acceptable. But it would soon be obvious to any newcomer that to try and operate other than on the tried and proven system which the Lobby had built up, and on which its existence depended, would be futile. There were occasions, however, where it would be clearly understood that the information which passed between the Lobby man and his informant was not to be released immediately but would be kept as background in readiness for when, after crosschecking the facts, it was felt by both parties that the time was right.

I have no doubt that, as with me, there are many stories which erstwhile colleagues have not disclosed and never will. In fact, some of these could have had a marked bearing and effect on British political history had they been written and published.

One particular instance springs to mind, in which I was personally involved soon after I had entered Westminster. During a late sitting I was in the Central Lobby making a last round-up when I was approached by Bill Coldrick, then one of the Bristol M.P.'s, whom I had become friendly with. In conversation he mentioned there was a backbench rumour that the government was facing some internal problem which involved a challenge to Prime Minister Attlee's leadership. So many "tips" of this kind and hints of Ministerial dissensions were being paraded that, unless one got names and reasons, they were treated as lobby-fodder and pure gossip.

It was sheeer coincidence that only a few minutes later who should appear but Jim Griffiths, M.P. for Llanelli and a Minister, though not a member of the Cabinet. I tackled him about the latest gossip and he surprised me by saying that he had heard there were some disloyal elements who were opposed to some proposal for a freeze on incomes and prices. Jim dismissed it all as another fiction and advised me not to run a hare which would make me and my paper look ridiculous. It was about the time that negotiations with America for the Marshall Aid plan were under way. The suggestion that a Labour government was contemplating a statutory prices and incomes freeze would undoubtedly have had serious repercussions at that time, not only on the U.S. talks but within the party ranks. After all, no government had ever attempted such a far-reaching political initiative.

In my inexperience at the time, I suppose, and also because of my respect for Jim and his reasoning, I took no action. Time was to show, however, that I had probably missed the biggest political story of my life. But in doing so I may well have saved the Attlee government, and the life-line for the British economy which is what Marshall Aid proved to be.

Forty years later it was confirmed to me that there *had* been substance in the 'gossip'. Clem Attlee had wanted a moratorium for six months on wage and price increases. Realising the probable effect of such action upon the party, and the repercussions on talks with the Americans, the Prime Minister called a few of his closest Ministers and advisers together to test their reaction before making it an issue for Cabinet. Ernest Bevin, Sir Stafford Cripps, and Herbert Morrison, the then Leader of the House of Commons, were names later associated with what was possibly the first example of the "Kitchen Committee" which afterwards became part of the makeup of every post-war government.

My confirmation came from Lord (formerly Sir Harold) Wilson during a recent chat in the House of Lords. He recalled that, at the time, when he was a Parliamentary Secretary, he had heard about the proposal, which had been treated with the utmost top secrecy. It had been dropped because Ernest Bevin, the Minister with the biggest following and strongest clout in the Labour party, would not be associated with it. It had remained a subject for discussion by the Attlee ad hoc committee and was never brought before the Cabinet. Consequently, it is not mentioned in the Cabinet memoranda and papers released under the Thirty-Years-Rule. "You are quite right," I was assured by Lord Wilson. "There *was* something in the tip-off you received, and Jim Griffiths did the government and the country a service when he persuaded you not to write about it." I still believe that Jim had no actual knowledge that a moratorium had been under consideration. Had he known anything positive he would not have discussed it with *me*!

I was taken under the wing of one of the kindest and most influential members of the Lobby, Guy Eden, then Political Correspondent of the *Daily Express*, who was also Honorary Secretary of the Lobby for many years. Within a few weeks I was one of his group, which also included Wilson Broadbent of the *Daily Mail*, and Guy's assistant, Robert Carvel, who eventually became Political Editor of the *London Evening Standard*. There were several of these groups and it was in this way that newspapers got a saturation coverage of the Westminster scene. How the groups worked was that each one would make its own contacts among Ministers and backbench M.P.'s. The "trawl" would be shared among members of the group and it would be up to each individual member to deal with any story or stories as he saw fit, and to follow up. There were the occasions, of course, when a scoop was picked up, in which case there was a recognised dispensation given by the rest, who would be informed only after the first or second edition times. But this did not happen too often.

One of the advantages of these groups' operations was that the various members had their own particular contacts in the various parties. When necessary these would be used either to substantiate information gleaned or to assess its impact in party-political terms. The system worked exceedingly well, as indeed it still does today.

As the newcomer I was expected to make my way with a little extra, but my strongest asset was that I had the car and the friendship of the Welsh Labour Group of M.P.'s, and in those days the Group included some of the most influential members of the Labour government.

Ipso facto, if anything involving Government policies was picked up in the "trawl", I was the one deputed to follow up. I would question my contacts and report back. Nye Bevan, in the early days of the Attlee government the Minister of Health and a very strong man in the Socialist movement, and Jim Griffiths, who was Minister for National Insurance, obviously were Ministers with whom the closest contact had to be kept. They were possibly the most influential members of the Attlee team at that time and in Lobby terms very hard nuts to crack. Throughout our association I would say they both behaved impeccably insofar as government and Labour Party issues were involved and never knowingly parted with or corroborated information to me on any highly confidential issues. "Knowingly" is the operative term.

I was also the chief Liberal party contact for our team because Clement Davies, M.P. for Montgomeryshire, was the Party Leader and the Liberals then, with more than a score of M.P.'s, formed an important part of the Opposition. They also had very strong Welsh affiliations.

Where stories involving the Conservative Party were concerned, Guy and Wilson were unbeatable in their standing with the Tories. Percy Cater, who worked in harness with Wilson Broadbent, was another member of the team and had the respect and confidence of M.P.'s on all sides of the House. So we had a closely-knit and influential force with sturdy feet in all camps and it paid off time and again. But it has to be remembered how different the Lobby then was from its present form.

Now there is more cut-and-thrust, and government information services via the Lobby seem to have taken away a lot of the
edge on Lobby reporting and investigative activities. For
instance, today almost everyone among our M.P.'s who has a
torch to carry or a theme or campaign to bring to the public
notice, provided it has some sort of political bearing, has easy
access to Lobby journalists through their officers.

It is a simple matter to request a meeting with Lobby Correspondents on any particular question, and a meeting-place or
committee-room is booked for it. Sometimes they pay off, but
more often they amount to nothing, owing to the pressures of
other more important or attractive stories and the shortage of
newspaper space. These, of course, are different from meetings
with the Lobby which are convened, with increasing frequency
it must be said, by official bodies of the main political parties.

Apart from the personal contacts which every Lobby Correspondent has to cultivate from Front and Back Benches and
which are the mainstream of the true Lobby stories, there are
meetings with Ministers and their Opposition counterparts,
known as "Shadows", whenever matters of government policy
are concerned which need to be brought to the public's attention. These are extremely important from the standpoint of
explanation and causes. Ministers will explain why a certain
Bill has to be introduced and what it proposes. Opposition
spokesmen invariably claim the right to a meeting to reveal
why this need not be, and seek to destroy or to diminish the
opponents' premise. But, as always, it is left to the Lobby journalists to form their own conclusions on causes and effects and
to see that these are what are passed on to their readers.

This system of Lobby calls took root in the immediate post-
war years. I recall some of my first Lobby meetings being convened at the behest of the then Leader of the House of Commons and Deputy Leader of the Labour Party, Herbert
Morrison. He was, possibly with the exception of "Rab"
Butler, who followed him for the Conservative government in

'The Radio Doctor'—Charles Hill, M.P.

1951, the finest political public-relations officer of any government. Some years later the Conservative government of Harold MacMillan laid such importance on the need to organise public relations from the centre that they made Luton M.P., Dr. Charles ("Radio Doctor") Hill, a Minister with specific responsibilites for government information. He had a great flair for this work, but I still rank Morrison and Butler as the greatest in this field insofar as the Lobby was concerned.

From the outset Morrison recognised the importance of the Lobby journalists' system and very quickly, and, in the politically, economically and socially difficult post-war reconstruction period, used it as the channel from Westminster to the people. Government policies had to be "sold" to a long-suffering public recovering from more than six years of war and facing its consequent upheavals. The government also had to be pretty sure, before launching some of the more controversial

policies which emerged after the 1945 General Election returned Labour with a landslide majority, that they would not cause
a major anti-government blowback.

So we had, on several occasions, meetings of the Lobby with
Herbert Morrison, or a chosen Minister, in the course of which
it would be slipped in that such and such a Bill was on the
stocks. This was a kind of handout which Lobby journalists
accepted gratefully at the beginning. Stories would be written
hinting at forthcoming legislation. The response fed back from
public reaction would be carefully analysed by Morrison and
his staff and others, and advices tendered to the responsible
policy-making body. It is known that several proposed measures deemed to be unpopular according to public reactions in
the Press were not proceeded with. Cabinet decisions reflecting
a turnaround on some major proposals have been registered.

This practice became known in Lobby circles as ''flying
government kites'' and did not last long once we realised we
were being duped. The Morrison technique lost its effect as the
Lobby members retaliated with their own game. We knew
when we were being used as Guinea Pigs and stories which
were dropped into our laps this way received a treatment which
began to reflect the deviousness of Administrations. ''Leaks''
were frequently blown up and caused considerable embarrassment to Downing Street. Internal inquiries often resulted and
it became recognised that a closer liaison with No. 10 would be
mutually beneficial.

The system of Downing Street Press Officers and staff,
appointed by the Prime Minister, was introduced by Clem
Attlee mainly at the instance of Herbert Morrison, and this developed into the regular daily contacts which have been maintained ever since. Like all things related to governments and
parliament, however, the system has developed over the years
and often nowadays receives wide recognition, as evidenced in
the Westland affair.

It was Herbert Morrison who regularised weekly meetings with the Lobby for "full and frank discussions, off the record" and exchanges of views. "Rab" Butler, his Tory Shadow, introduced Opposition follow-up meetings, usually within the hour. These became institutionalised as "the meetings that never took place". They were never openly referred to from either side and they led to such phrases in reports as "sources close to the government" or "according to official sources" and "official quarters".

The practice has been preserved with some changes. Perhaps the biggest of these is that movement within the Lobby/government circle has become more widely detectable, and even openly referred to at Westminster and Whitehall. Those who are in day-by-day contact with the Press coverage at Westminster have no illusions any longer that "government spokesman" or "sources close to government" refer to Lobby meetings with appointed spokesmen entrusted to pass on the official comment on any particular issue of the day.

Originally Lobby meetings and contacts were non-attributable. Lobby journalists would not be noticed leaving the Members' Lobby or the corridors for a particular venue—usually a small room on the top floor of the Palace, overlooking the Thames and Westminster Bridge—because they just melted away in small numbers. Nowadays it would more likely resemble a miniature cavalry charge and then the participants would find themselves packed like sardines into a room which was intended to hold less than half the present Lobby strength.

Whereas, in my earlier days, it was expressly forbidden to discuss any Lobby activity with another in the presence or within the earshot of an M.P. or any "outsider" on penalty of being brought before "the committee", this seems no longer to obtain. How can it when M.P.'s seem so much aware of what the Lobby is up to or has been hearing? By attracting so much attention in various ways the original mystique has vanished.

The facilities remain, but the magic aura of the special relationships of elected Members and Peers with Lobby journalists has
been irrevocably tarnished. More is the pity, and inevitably this
situation presents the greatest threat to a unique and necessary
system.

The history of parliamentary and political reporting is a fascinating story which should have as great an appeal to the
populace as to the student. After all, politics is about people and
what happens at Westminster touches upon each one of us. Yet
it seems that very little is known about the principle and the
means through which information about the activities of Parliament and our elected representatives is made known
publicly.

The two institutions, the Parliamentary Press Gallery and
the Lobby Journalists, have been in existence for just over a
hundred years—only a short while in comparison with the
eight hundred years of what the world knows as The Mother of
Parliaments. Our Parliament, however, secured its constitutional supremacy only in 1698, and our Constitution remains an
unwritten one.

Not so many, I imagine, are aware that the open reporting of
Parliament over the past century was won only after a hard, and
often vicious, battle gainst Statute and red tape. Nor will there
be many who will know that reporting or published commentary was forbidden by law until comparatively recently. Not
until 1972, in fact, did an enlightened government under the
Premiership of Edward Heath abolish the Statute, which had
fallen into disuse and disrepute. With the full support of both
Houses of Parliament, the Heath government removed the
criminal taint from which Parliamentary reporters and com-
mentators had suffered (albeit with indifference) in their
disregard of the law.

Freedom of thought and speech are the main tenets of our
Constitution, yet the reporting of affairs which touched on the
nation's very existence had remained taboo for centuries. Of

course, no one within our democratic institution would have attempted to arraign these correspondents, and this alone made an ass of the law. The folly of it all, therefore, was that no one had attempted to revoke it sooner.

Freedom has been restored lawfully, but those who work at Westminster are not conscious of any difference! Freedom, that is, within the bounds of Parliamentary privilege as regards commenting on the work of Parliament and its elected Members.

There is one notable exception, and one which is jealously guarded by M.P.'s and governments of the day: no-one may report a Secret Session of Parliament. The institution of a Secret Session is a throwback from the days of Charles I and the necessity forced upon the House of Commons at that time to hide from the Sovereign the state of the national coffers. A rule was made that, with the consent of its Members, the House of Commons could go into secret session, and it was also decided that anyone responsible for revealing any information about the proceedings would suffer dire penalties. Only those elected to the House of Commons had the privilege of attending and any breach of privilege could mean an extreme punishment. That rule has been sustained down the years.

Secret Sessions, however, are a rare occurrence. On only three occasions during my forty-odd years had the House of Commons voted itself this right . . . and during one of them I put myself into a situation of gross breach of privilege. It happened during the fiasco of the Suez ''war'' in 1956 when Sir Anthony Eden's government ordered the attack against Egypt's President Nasser over the Suez Canal issue, and the hostilities fizzled out with a tremendous loss of face for the British. It was a situation about which Winston Churchill, who had handed the Premiership over to Sir Anthony, was to comment later that he would never have dared to be drawn into such a commitment, but if he had, he would not have dared to stop!

The House of Commons sat behind closed and guarded doors. From the Press Gallery corridor behind the Chamber could be heard occasional outbursts as a volatile Opposition attacked the Eden policy. The hours rolled by and I and my colleagues were seething with frustration. There was a good story to be told; the world was awaiting anxiously the outcome of the debate, but we had no facts to report. It was in this frame of mind that I recall taking a stroll down to the Members' Lobby. With so much hubbub inside the Chamber it was not surprising to find the Lobby deserted, except for the Badge Messengers and the custodian of the locked door into the Chamber.

Suddenly I became aware of Colonel Marcus Lipton, the Labour M.P. for Battersea, an old and trusted confidant. He was very angry. My impression was that he had either failed to "catch the Speaker's eye", as M.P.'s say when they are seeking to be called upon to speak, or he had been given the brush-off by some of his colleagues. I suspected it was the former, but since no record of secret proceedings is ever published it is impossible to know exactly. Either way, the Colonel was in the mood to talk, and talk he did to someone who must have been his most avid listener of all time.

I guided him into the Library Corridor, away from possible peeking eyes, and just let him blow off steam. He gave me virtually a blow-by-blow account of what was happening behind the closed doors and I lapped it up. This was the stuff that scoops were made of! Like me, I do not think he was fully aware that what he was giving out was strictly taboo. It was, as he reminded me, "on Lobby terms", which meant that the source of the information rested only between the two of us. So carried away was I by this windfall of highly descriptive accounts and comments that I broke one of the Lobby's cardinal rules—never to be seen scribbling in or around the Lobby when speaking to a Member. My pocket notebook was quickly being exhausted. Looking back all those years it seems to me now I was lucky it did not burst into flames as Marcus expanded on the various clashes on the floor of the House.

There was no time to type out the exclusive story I intended to file. I scribbled a few notes of guidance on the back of the day's Order Paper, earmarked some quotes and off I scarpered to the Press Gallery and a telephone. I had dialled through to my paper in Cardiff, and even spoken to the News Desk (as was usual before a big story was filed) when Guy Eden, the *Daily Express* political correspondent and my early mentor in the Lobby poked his head around the door of the telephone-box. "What's happening?" he asked, obviously attracted by my ill-concealed impatience to get the story through. I must have been the only active journalist in sight at that moment, and the question was perfectly justified. After all, we were working more often than not as a team. "Only a leak from the debate and it's all good stuff," I answered. "I'll pass it on afterwards." Guy reached out and depressed the telephone hook.

"What the . . ." I began to remonstrate. Guy was an awfully good chap, always quiet, polite and well spoken. I'd never seen him in a temper nor even in a bad mood, so it was only when he said sharply, "You've been here long enough to know better!" that I realised I had put my foot in it. What he had done, in fact, was to save me from the frightening experience of having to answer to the House of Commons for an unmitigated breach of privilege, and even more. He must have saved my career. The seriousness of what I had nearly done was brought home to me later, when a lesser breach was unwittingly committed by another Lobby Correspondent. I have no doubt now that, had my story appeared, my sojourn at Westminster would have been pretty brief thereafter. I never forgot how much I owed Guy Eden for that. I'm only sorry he died so tragically from a heart attack in the prime of life.

Chapter 5: How it all began

Why, it may be asked, was the strange law forbidding any reporting of Parliamentary activities passed in the first place? The experts tell us it dated back from the time before Parliamentary democracy in the form we now know it came to this country.

In those days ordinary individuals just took orders from their superiors. It was left to the higher-ups to run things without any interference. From their point of view as administrators it was better that how they ran things should be kept as quiet and as restricted as possible. Obviously this could not be achieved if the doings of Parliament were made known to the public in general. Those, of course, were the days before newspapers; but then some public-spirited persons started issuing pamphlets which evoked public interest. And why not? Were these not informing them about matters which concerned and affected them?

It was from that time that the people became more inquisitive about what was taking place in Parliament, and questions began being asked. The rule against revealing the affairs of Parliament, which until then had seemed adequate enough, now had to be tightened up. The records show that until 1770 Parliament decreed it to be a breach of privilege, carrying severe penalties, for the public to be given any account of the views of Members of Parliament, particularly those expressed on the Floor of the House of Commons. What was being carried on in Parliament was being kept a close secret, ostensibly so that the Sovereign should not know. But then nobody on the outside could get to know either!

The crunch came in 1771. A City of London printer had the temerity, or courage, to publish a report of a speech made by an M.P. and the matter was raised in the House of Commons. There was a demand that the offender should be arrested and arraigned for a breach of Parliamentary privilege. The then Lord

Mayor, supported by City dignitaries, led a procession down the Strand and towards Westminster as a mass protest. This was probably the first attempted "lobbying" of M.P.'s in Parliament's history, but it availed the imprisoned printer nothing. The sovereign right of Parliament was upheld.

The unfortunate Lord Mayor was committed to the Tower of London until the end of the parliamentary session and there he remained for about six weeks. That was just over two hundred years ago and technically the same, or an even more severe, penalty could be exacted by Parliament today for any proven breach of its privileges. Factually, however, in these more enlightened days, to attempt such retribution would call down on the heads of our administrators the wrath of a public which is being spoon-fed with increasing doses of parliamentary and political information. Nonetheless there still exists a parallel to incarceration in the Tower. When any "stranger" (which is the term applied by the elected Members to any member of the public visible from the Floor of the House, that is to say in any of the public galleries) causes a disturbance within the Chamber and is forthwith ejected, it is usual for the Serjeant at Arms, who is responsible for the well-being of our M.P.'s and security when the House is sitting, to order the miscreant's detention in the police cell beneath Big Ben until the rising of the House or, where there has been a serious attempt at disrupting the proceedings of Parliament or attacking M.P.'s, until such time as the House of Commons can decide what penalty must be exacted. In this respect it must be remembered that Parliament is the highest court in the land, with undisputed powers.

Despite the attempted mass lobbying of 1771, it continued to be unlawful to report the proceedings of Parliament. But as public interest, already whetted by secret publications, increased (and, one suspects, as would happen in these days, that the Lord Mayor's demonstration served only to accentuate public awareness of a vital shortcoming in public affairs) the reporting ban was sidestepped without further serious repercussions. Fictitious reports in the third person appeared in the magazines and broadsheets of the day.

In the House itself there appeared the forerunners of the modern columnists. These were "The Memory Men" who attended from time to time in the public galleries. They were in the pay of some of the more adventurous printers and there is a reference to one of them in particular. Known as "Memory Woodfall", he was reputed to be able to repeat the whole of a debate in sequence without the help of a single note. It was to be another fifty years before the open reporting of Parliament began.

The persecution of those who dared in various ways to drive the proverbial horse and cart through the law continued. There are records of several authors of articles purporting to be jottings of House of Commons debates being severely dealt with. And yet they persevered.

Among the earliest reporters of Parliamentary debates was Dr. Johnson. He was then about thirty years of age and, taken from surreptitiously scribbled notes in the public gallery, his reports appeared in *The Gentlemen's Magazine* under the title *"The Senate of Lilliput"*. No real names were used and many of the jottings had to be from memory because there was no shorthand in those days.

Not until the advent of Charles Dickens at the age of twenty was shorthand used for reporting. Samuel Pepys, of *Diary* fame, had produced a one-off form of shorthand used only by him, but it is Dickens who is now proudly proclaimed by the Press Gallery as the first full-time verbatim parliamentary reporter.

With the continuing growth of public interest in parliamentary affairs it was inevitable that some facility should be sought for those who had to sit in the public gallery making rough notes with notepads on their knees. In 1831 the House of Lords agreed to the setting-up of a Press Gallery which was no more than granting facilities for note-taking. It was not until 1834 that the House of Commons followed suit.

The Press Gallery as an official body of parliamentary journalists was instituted in the House of Lords in 1847 and in the House of Commons in 1852. The facilities were still sparse and related only to note-taking. Another thirty years had to pass before the Parliamentary Press Gallery emerged in its present format and in 1882 provincial newspapers were admitted.

Things now are vastly different from the days when Charles Dickens complained of having to stand ''in a preposterous pen'' to record the debates in the House of Lords. He also wrote ''I have worn my knees out by writing on them in the back row of the old Gallery of the House of Commons''.

Although that was more than eighty years before I began my period in the House, I can, in a way, lay claim to be the last one in the Press Gallery to have a kind of direct link with Dickens, the acknowledged ''Father of the Press Gallery''. It happened, a few months after my accreditation, that one day I was asked to make room on the Lobby bench in the House of Lords. At that time the House of Lords Chamber was being used by the M.P.'s whilst the House of Commons, which had been destroyed by the Luftwaffe in the 1940 blitz, was being rebuilt. Several of the Lobby journalists had been allotted seats alongside the Distinguished Gallery. I was very surprised when an aged gentleman was ushered in by an attendant and sat next to me. He was Sir Alexander Mackintosh, then aged 93 and still on the Parliamentary Press Gallery list.

His visits were few and brief and invariably he would drop off during Question Time. When he began to snore, it was I who would gently nudge him awake. I used to feel very embarrassed because sometimes his snoring could be heard on the Floor of the House and I was conscious of the upward glances of some Members. For about two months Sir Alex would come to the House at least once a week and in that time we became better acquainted. He would tell me of his early days in the Gallery,

towards the end of Dickens' sojourn, and that he had known the
great man, whom he described as "awesome in appearance and
manner" to other reporters who were allowed into the House.
Eventually I began to sense a direct association with Charles
Dickens which grew stronger with each chat with Sir Alex, who
somehow had taken to me. It may have been because of those
gentle nudges, but I gathered he seldom spoke to anyone else.
He had joined the Press Gallery very young, before the 1870's,
but whether as a cub-reporter I do not know. He was its Chairman in 1927 when he was the Parliamentary Correspondent for
the *Liverpool Daily Post.*

Brief as our friendship was, it became one of the most treasured experiences of my earlier days and I missed our chats very
much. I only wish we had met much earlier so I could have been
more fully informed about the Dickens era and the formative
years of the Press Gallery. One thing was obvious, however,
Dickens' awesome appearance and manner had remained with
Sir Alex to the end.

There are no records to show just how few were that first
band of parliamentary reporters in 1847. Sufficient to point out,
however, that today the Press Gallery alone has a complement
of more than three hundred and the Lobby (whose members are
also members of the Gallery) has about half that number
accredited by the Serjeant at Arms, who is responsible to the
House of Commons for the affiliations and the administration
within the precincts of Westminster of that august body.

Nowhere in any of the world's governments, even in those
which are patterned on the Mother of Parliaments, will be
found insitutions with such unique associations and relationships. Whilst this continues in the responsible manner in
which both the Lobby and the Gallery conduct their respective
obligations to Parliament and the people so will British democracy be safeguarded and sustained.

Chapter 6: Smoke-room Secrets

The title "Lobby Correspondent" gives the clue to a special status enjoyed in the normal conduct of parliamentary affairs. Of all the Westminster-based journalists, he or she is the only one privileged to mix with M.P.'s and members of the House of Lords on their own stamping-grounds, namely the Lobbies which are exclusive to both Houses, and the corridors which have been so aptly described as "The Corridors of Power". Only a few places are out of bounds to the Lobby Correspondent. The M.P.'s Library, their Smoking-Room, the Speaker's Corridor and Behind the Chair and Division Lobbies, and their Dining and Tea-Rooms are the main areas. In these the Members have complete privacy away from the continuous peering gazes and the keen hearing of those who, in a sense, supervise the happenings in Parliament.

Still, many Lobby Correspondents get to know an awful lot of what takes place within those private areas. There are always some people who, whether to curry favour or to get back at their own or the other side, are ready to pass on into the daily grinding-machine a morsel or two which, at the end of the day, becomes the gossip paragraph or even the front-page lead.

I myself have been on the receiving end of some of these. For instance the occasion when Winston Churchill was approached by his Chief Whip, Patrick Buchan-Hepburn, in the Members' Smoking-Room and told he should hurry back into the Chamber where he was under fierce attack by Tom Driberg, Labour M.P. for Barking. With a typically Churchillian reaction, the then Leader of the Opposition, as I was informed, muttered something into his whisky and turned round with the acid comment, "Driberg? Isn't that the chap who brought sodomy into disrepute?" The old man knew exactly whom Buchan-Hepburn was talking about, but he could not resist getting one across about the occasion when it was alleged Driberg had been found in a compromising situation with a male driver whilst he was attached to the War Commission in Germany after the war.

The Smoke-Room also was the favourite haunt of a powerful group of Labour M.P.'s, the academics and professional politicians, which produced a virulent and potent strain of Member, each of whom in turn, and as a group, made a lasting impression upon and contribution to the post-war Labour Party, both within the House of Commons and in the country. Among their ranks were Nye Bevan, Anthony Crosland, Dick Crossman, Barbara Castle, Tom Driberg and the two survivors still at the Commons, namely Michael Foot and Tony Benn. There were others, of course, but these were the ones within the epicentre, as it were, of dissent over socialist ideals, (or what they regarded as socialist ideals) not being embraced by the Parliamentary Labour Party. It was mainly from them that the constant rumblings emerged and they also devised many of the strategies for the Floor of the House.

They had many enemies on both sides of the House and consequently the ''leaks'' from their conversations and deliberations in the Smoke-Room frequently found their way to Lobby Correspondents. A favourite occupation—not a pastime, as I was once assured by Dick Crossman during one of the private Garrick Club lunches he used to hold when he was Leader of the House of Commons—was to discuss tactics prior to a major debate and to think up catch-phrases calculated to catch the ears and imagination of the journalists in the Press Gallery. These exercises paid off, time and again. Members of this ''think-tank'' are on record for powerful speeches made in the House on major occasions, and study of them, if they could be comprehensively compiled, would reveal the adept use of phrases which hit the headlines and gave much more publicity to the speeches than they would otherwise have attracted.

There is one memorable phrase which will forever remain in my mind. It was one of Nye Bevan's. He was winding up a debate as Opposition spokesman, attacking the Tory government's Health-Service proposals. With typical Bevan fervour, and pointing an accusing finger at the Front Bench, he claimed he had "burst their bladder of lies with the Poniard of Truth". It had been good hefty debating and swingeing attacks finely laced with scornful wit by the greatest exponent of the art, but it was this peroration that brought down the House. Later I was told that that particular phrase had been created during the previous evening's session in the Smoking-Room.

There were many instances of this particular exploitation, and it seemed Nye Bevan had more successes than the others, possibly because of his more clinical technique and his particular brand of oratory, with its commanding vocabulary. Nowadays the art of oratory on the Floor of the House is more conspicuous by its absence. It seems a thing of the past. That is not to say that some M.P.'s cannot still make contributions which can hold the House, but nowadays the speeches are different. There is a heavier accent on party politics, and unpolished invective is flung across the floor in the bid to score party points. This may seem more effective in modern circumstances, but there are very few among contemporary M.P.'s who can command the attention of the House when they get up to speak, and in so doing command world attention too. It must not be forgotten that the proceedings of the British Parliament are constantly under the world's searchlights and its utterances are carefully monitored.

One who seemed to have little time for the "thinkers" at that time was George Brown, destined to become the most controversial of Britain's Foreign Secretaries in this century. It may have been that in those days he did not frequent the Smoke-Room as frequently as happened in later years. He also had ambitions under Gaitskell and became deputy leader of the party in 1960. Ironically it was Wilson who went on in 1963 to the leadership when George's challenge failed and he remained the deputy.

The corridor between the Members' Lobby and the Library, out of bounds to other than Lobby Correspondents, was the favourite stalking ground for the Lobby. If one waited long enough it was virtually certain that the Lobby Correspondent would pick up a story or two in conversation with M.P.'s who constantly traversed the corridor to and from the Chamber. I remember one day Dick Crossman had stopped to talk to me— I cannot remember whether it was about some specific matter or just a friendly "how do". George Brown swept out of the tea-room and remarked in passing, "Careful, Boyo . . . they're up to something . . ." I took it to mean Dick and his colleagues were "in session" in the Smoke-Room. He snapped back at George and then stumped off in a huff, when a jovial Quintin Hogg, who had paused, grinned and said, "My dog sings better . . ." I was very friendly then with the future Lord Chancellor Hailsham and the only story I got out of the incident was from him. "It's true, you know," he remarked. "My dog (I forget his name) sings 'Men of Harlech' a treat when I play it on the piano." It was good as a gossip snippet, but the exchange between George Brown and Dick Crossman was indicative of the mistrust in which the "think-tank" was held in some quarters.

I had a soft spot for George Brown and was sorry to see him hitting the bottle so hard as he moved up the Front Bench pecking-order. But I believe the thing which really increased his drinking was his period as the First Secretary and Secretary of State for Economic Affairs in the Wilson government between 1964 and 1966. In partnership with Jim Callaghan, Chancellor of the Exchequer, he had the problem of formulating an incomes policy as the first tenet of the Labour government to the background of a "Tory legacy of an £800 million balance of payments deficit." The pressures began showing more evidently as this two years' burden continued. The biggest surprise to those of us who were privy to George's drinking bouts was his appointment as Foreign Secretary in 1966, and it was during the early part of this period in office that I became personally involved in this most embarrassing situation.

Unfortunately stories about his performances under the influence at home and abroad gained steady currency at Westminster and in Whitehall, and this was something to which the Prime Minister could not turn a blind eye indefinitely. Poor George! He was a benevolent and capable politician who turned out to be another sad chapter in the Westminster story. His elevation to the Peerage, however, was no more than a just reward, and it brought with it a more temperate personage. Lord George Brown, despite his major failing, sustained the vast respect which he had unquestionably earned in his younger days in the Labour Party. His death was sincerely mourned on all sides.

Chapter 7: Eat, Drink and be merry

Sir William Steward, who was then M.P. for West Woolwich, one of the London constituencies, is someone who deserves special mention in the post-war records of the House of Commons. A restaurateur and owner of the famous London Indian Restaurant, Veraswamy's, he was Chairman of the Commons Kitchen Committee between 1951 and 1955. He had undertaken to make the House of Commons catering arrangements self-supporting at least during that period.

This was unthinkable at the time. For a great many years the expense of feeding M.P.'s and authorised officials at Westminster had been a terrible strain on the Treasury, which was obliged to make up deficits which mounted every year. Until Bill Steward came along, the M.P.'s meals were heavily subsidised, and it was something the taxpayer looked to be stuck with for the foreseeable future, especially since the Labour government of 1945-51 had decreed that the Catering Wages Act should apply to the Royal Palace of Westminster as well as to other Palaces.

As a Royal Palace, Westminster is outside all licensing laws and there hours did not matter. And as the House of Commons could not operate within set hours, especially during the days of Labour's grand nationalisation plans, when M.P.'s, in committee and in the Chamber, were often in constant session for longer than a day, it was necessary that catering arrangements should be provided at all sorts of irregular hours. Although M.P.'s paid for their meals at prices equal to those of outside restaurants, the gap between revenue and overheads was horrendous, and with each year it increased.

In such conditions it was claimed that House of Commons catering could never be run without heavy losses. That was until Bill Steward came along. He was a professional, of course, and given a free hand he guaranteed it could be done within his four-year stewardship. He did it by applying business methods which increased efficiencies and enabled M.P.'s to eat just as well at the same or at only slightly higher cost to themselves.

It left a legacy, however, which grew and grew and which has changed the face and image of Westminster. For the first time the public were allowed, on M.P.'s sponsorship, to book, at somewhat inflated prices, rooms within the Palace for social occasions. The idea was cultivated by successive Kitchen Committees and today it is commonplace to find as many, if not more, outsiders dining at Westminster as incumbents themselves, even on sitting days. During recesses, of course, the trade is even better. But the costs are met, and the Treasury has long since ceased to worry about the Commons Catering Estimates and the subsidy. It all began with Bill Steward's almost superhuman feat which, I suggest, merits a mention in Westminster records if not in the Guinness Book of Records.

It was during Bill's chairmanship that Winston Churchill's eightieth birthday was celebrated, and the House of Commons honoured the great man. I was one of two Lobby Correspondents (the other was Barney Keelan of the *Eastern Daily Press*) invited by Bill, later Sir William, to witness the final tapping of an enormous barrel of Sherry by Gonzalez Byass. It took place at their Bonded Stores in Old Thames Street, as I recall.

The Sherry had been laid down in the year of Churchill's birth and there was just sufficient left to allow a bottle for each of the eighty years. The eighty bottles were displayed in private because it was intended as a complete surprise for the wartime leader. A few extra were put on one side, and it was from one of these that we were allowed a taster. It was nectar! Sheer bliss to roll over the tongue and swallow slowly, with a lingering ecstacy.

As I drove Bill and Barney back to the Commons I casually mentioned something about giving a right arm to get a bottle of the Old Methuselah. A couple of days later there was a cryptic note on my desk from the Chairman of the Kitchen Committee. I was to go to his room (where Annie's Bar is now) and there

I would find something about which I was not to breathe a word to anyone—and I haven't until now! I did as I was instructed and in his top-drawer was what must have been one of the few extra O.M.'s. Yes, there it was, worth its weight in gold! But it didn't end there.

I was determined not to open that bottle except for a very, very, special occasion, and this happened on a January day a couple of years later. Our elder son, David, announced his engagement, the first in our family. This was it! It was why that special bottle had been nestling in the back of the cabinet for two years. Aged and opaque, it was to me something no one else could have offered. With increasing excitement I groped for it. Panic . . . No bottle . . . Then the casual explanation from Myfanwy. Christmas had been approaching: she needed a drop of sherry for the pudding; there was this old bottle to hand . . . But even worse . . . The milkman, the baker's roundsman and even the window-cleaner ("He was very cold and shivering"), chanced about that very time to make their pre-Christmas call. They would relish a Christmas drink. Oh, the irony of it all; the window cleaner came back after his chore and hinted at another sip. And, the last drop drunk, the bottle was relegated to the dustbin. Only the poor refuse-man, it seemed, had not sampled the liquid gold.

Not one of them could have known that on that Christmas, 1959, they had sipped what only a Prime Minister of Britain could have got from his cellar. It was catastrophe, but we got over it.

A few years later I told the story to an old friend, Major Miller of Dean's Yard, a cousin of the author, Daphne Du Maurier, and reputedly an authority on wines. His face blanched. He was obviously suffering a mental paroxysm as his mind registered the milkman, the baker's roundsman and the window-cleaner (twice) quaffing the precious liquid without discrimination or taste. "Are you still married to THAT woman?" he croaked, adding that it could make the theme for a good story. Yes, we had been married thirty-one years then, and are still, and happily, after forty-eight years. But we would both very much have liked to have had a drop of that nectar. It would have been, for me, another worthwhile perk of the job.

Chapter 8: Breach of Privilege

It has been my lot during my years in the Lobby to have been the confidant of many, and witness to scores of events which in small or large measure, have played a part in post-war British history. Many of these events will remain untold so long as there is any possibility of disclosure being to the detriment of those concerned. Otherwise, I think the time has come to share some of them as matters of general interest. Breach of Parliamentary privilege was, and remains, the nightmare of a Lobby Correspondent and my first recollection of such a breach concerned the famous budget-leak of then Chancellor of the Exchequer, Hugh Dalton. I had been at Westminster less than six months, and was attending the first of what would be more than fifty Budgets (including the mini-budgets which became almost a way of life during Dennis Healey's term as Chancellor of the Exchequer).

It was the practice in those days for the Chancellor to open his Budget with a state-of-the-nation's-economy statement at about 3.30 p.m. For the next half hour there would be a general analysis of the economic situation. Because of the effects of Budget changes, especially taxation, on the Stock Exchange, every Chancellor had to keep a careful eye on the clock. The Stock Exchange closed at four o'clock and not until a few minutes after that time would there be any hint from the Despatch Box of what was in store for taxpayers. On that particular day Hugh Dalton was in a happy mood as he draped his six-foot-plus figure around the Despatch Box. His quips in a loud booming voice, and his chuckles as he toyed mentally with some thought or other, gave no hint of what was about to burst upon him. As I recall, he cheerfully told the House that he had a song in his heart as he poured out the preamble to his budget proposals. Although other versions of exactly what happened differ in some respects, and especially in suggesting that it was not until the following day that the bombshell burst, I still remember an outburst from the Conservative Benches shortly after the actual Budget proposals had been revealed and that it caused me at the time to think it was more than the usual Opposition rejoinders on these occasions. Many years later, Nigel Birch told me that the hint of a leak in one of the London evening papers had been flashed down the backbenches from no-one was certain where, and this was what had started the row which excited Tories sought to precipitate. It fizzled out, however, and not until the following day was Dalton called upon to explain in the House "a leak to the *London Star*".

The commotion on the Opposition benches was spearheaded by a group who called themselves "The Harriers". They included the present Lord Chancellor, Lord Hailsham (who was then Quintin Hogg), Peter Thorneycroft, then M.P. for Monmouth and who was to become a Chancellor of the Exchequer (and around whom the Macmillan government tottered in 1958 when he and two of his Treasury Ministers, Enoch Powell and Nigel Birch, resigned over expenditure cuts), David Eccles— known on the backbenches as "Fancy Boots"—and the said Nigel Birch. They got their name because of a pledge to harry and harass the Attlee government at every opportunity. The commotion I had heard must have been the Group in action, but it could not have been over the leak. Had they become aware that the *Star's* forecast of what the Budget contained was to be treated as a direct Budget leak they would have created much more than they did on that afternoon.

From subsequent statements and the Inquiry it was certain that Dalton had no idea when he was on his feet of any impending trouble. Not until late on Budget Day, when he heard from his Treasury Minister, Douglas Jay, in the first instance, and later from Herbert Morrison, Leader of the House, and the Prime Minister, did he realise the gravity of his predicament. And it had happened so innocently!

The Chancellor had stopped to talk very briefly to John Carvel, Political Correspondent of *The Star*, as he was approaching the Members' Lobby on his way into the crowded House. M.P.'s at that time were occupying the House of Lords Chamber, and the approach to the Lobby was along the corridor leading from the M.P.'s Dining-Room. He simply answered an innocuous question about what he intended to use as the Chancellor's traditional drink during the Budget. Unfortunately he had embellished his reply with some hint and although *The Star*—like other newspapers—had given a pretty accurate forecast, John hardened his story later. The Attlee Inquiry showed later that this had had no effect or impact on any Stock Exchange dealings.

Later I was to learn the unfortunate train of events from John himself, Willie Alison (the Political Correspondent of the other London evening paper, the *Evening Standard*, on whose behalf John had questioned Dalton about the drink) and from Lobby Secretary, Guy Eden. Quite rightly, John was exonerated from any malpractice or deliberate Breach of Privilege, but the gruelling experience for even such a seasoned Lobby man took toll of his health for some time.

How the matter came to a head with a Parliamentary Question on the day after the Budget by Tory M.P., Victor Raikes, how Dalton offered his resignation immediately Attlee had summoned the Inner Cabinet to discuss the situation, and his replacement by Sir Stafford Cripps, who became the Austere Chancellor, is amply recorded. It is the unknown sequel I am now prompted to reveal.

In his superb biography of Dalton it is claimed by Ben Pimlott that, after his visit to the Palace to tender his Seals of Office to the King, Dalton left No. 11 Downing Street, the Chancellor's official residence, to be taken to dinner by two friends, John Wilmot, who had just been sacked as Minister of Supply, and Nigel Davenport. He did not return to stay with Ruth, his wife, perhaps, as Ben Pimlott explains, because their relationship had been strained for some time. By this time the Prime Minister had announced an inquiry into the incident, and Dalton's dismissal.

The ex-Chancellor had not been well and the new pressures must have been the final stroke because he disappeared from the Parliamentary scene. In Lobby circles, still buzzing with speculation about the aftermath, it was known that some concern was being expressed about Dalton's disappearance. His wife knew nothing, and there were hints that Special Branch officers had been alerted. Enquiries at his Bishop Auckland constituency in Durham shed no light on his whereabouts. Rumours became rife.

It was mid-November and the weather was not good, but Dalton seemed to have disappeared from the face of the earth. Little appeared in the papers, partly, I suppose, because the government inquiry was about to get under way.

About a week after Budget Day, late one evening, I received a telephone call from Dai Grenfell, then Labour M.P. for Gower. He wondered whether I could come to the Welsh Room to give my opinion and some help on an autobiography he was writing. The Welsh Room is a little-known room off Westminster Hall. It had been known as such for many years, since only Welsh M.P.'s ever used it. It is so small that it could not accommodate the Welshman's penchant for committee meetings, not even on a small scale, and therefore, except by some of the older M.P.'s, it was seldom used.

We were bent over some pages of handwritten script when the door opened. The room was only dimly lit and it was difficult to make out who had come in, the door being in a recess leading to the Hall. *Someone* lurched in. For a moment I was nonplussed. Whoever he was, he was tall and very much under the influence of drink. He had on an old black homburg and a raincoat which looked as though it had been dragged through mud.

I remember vividly Dai's reaction . . . ''Arglwydd Mawr!'' (Good God), he said, as he clutched at the unsteady figure. It was then I recognised it as Hugh Dalton. Speaking in Welsh, Dai told me to take the other side and between us we helped him through the door. Dalton slurred something which sounded like . . . "The bloody Press". He must have recognised me, because a few weeks earlier I had interviewed him about his family connections with Neath. His maternal grandparents had lived in The Gnoll and Hugh had been born there. His father was a priest of the Church of England. Years later young Dalton moved with the family to Windsor, where his father became Canon and officiated for the Royal Family.

What a ludicrous scene it must have been in Westminster Hall (fortunately not well lit either) with two short persons propping up a 6ft 6 inch inebriate as they made their stumbling way towards the exit and the taxi-rank.

Bob, the policeman who knew every member and officer of the House of Commons, showed no signs of recognition or surprise as he waved up one of the waiting cabs into which he helped us to pour the gangly Dalton. Dai pushed me back and hissed, "If you say anything about this I'll bloody kill you!" Of course he didn't mean it, but I had had some encounters with Dai already and I knew how formidable he could be.

I returned to the Press Gallery, for it was pretty late, but I could still have made the London edition. And it was a story which would have got the headlines, not a fudge paragraph. However, I had given my word. I did keep my mouth shut, albeit with an uneasy conscience; the rule of the Lobby was too strong within me.

When I saw Dai Grenfell the following morning all he would say was, "Thanks. Mrs Dalton was glad to know he was all right." No mention of where he had taken him, but I noticed that he looked as though he had been up at least half the night. I wondered afterwards whether it was loyalty on Dai's part towards his former boss, because in 1940 Dalton had been made President of the Board of Trade and one of his three junior Ministers was Dai, as Minister for Mines. If it *was* loyalty, perhaps he would not have felt the same had he known that Dalton, as was revealed in his biography, had regarded him as stupid and incompetent in the job and had tried to sack him. He was prevented from doing so by Attlee, then deputy to Prime Minister Churchill. He had a soft spot for Dai who, he knew, had the confidence of Labour's mining M.P.'s.

The incident was never raised between us again, but, re-searching it, I came across the letter which Attlee sent to Dalton on November 13th, 1947. Typical of the Prime Minister, it was brief and to the point. "My dear Chancellor," it says, "when you informed me of yesterday's incident, you immediately offered me your resignation and you have now written to me formally. I have given the matter my earnest consideration and have come to the conclusion, with great regret, that it is my duty to accept it. I realise that this indiscretion in itself did not result in any action detrimental of the State; but the principle of the inviolability of the Budget is of the highest importance, and the discretion of the Chancellor of the Exchequer, who necessarily receives many confidential communications, must be beyond question.

"I need not tell you how painful it is to me to have to lose an old and valued colleague whose services to the government have been so great. I sympathise with you very deeply in this interruption to a distinguished career . . .".

The word "interruption" was prophetic enough. Dalton made his comeback under Attlee as Chancellor of the Duchy of Lancaster, and then as Minister for Local Government and Planning, but he never climbed back to top Ministerial rank or again assumed any meaningful power in the Party ranks.

*   *   *

There were times when I thought the incident in the Welsh Room *had* rubbed off on Dalton because, on his return to Ministerial Office about a year later, he showed me much courtesy and friendliness. So much so that he became my guest at the annual Lobby Lunch at the Savoy Hotel. This was the social event of the year in the Parliamentary calendar, and one for which there was very keen competition among M.P.'s for an invitation from their Lobby Correspondents. It was also an event which "never took place". No reference was made to it publicly and no reports appeared of it in the Press or on the B.B.C. Only once was this strict rule broken, and the offender was a well-known daily gossip-columnist who had been invited by his colleague to the function. When he turned up, he was made aware of the Lobby's anger. He was never invited again.

The Lobby Lunch was a "Debrett" occasion for the politicians. Every available member of the government, led by the Prime Minister, attended, as did the Opposition also. With a capacity of about 350, as many M.P.'s and Peers as possible were also invited—small wonder that competition for invitations was so keen! That it was held under the usual Lobby terms meant that the top-table speeches were not only informal but usually informative. I heard some vintage Churchill, Macmillan, Attlee and Wilson speeches—and several others in their time—and it was a great shame that the event had to end, mainly because of its cost. Not many of the present Lobby members have had the opportunity of attending the annual Lobby Lunch.

However, on this particular occasion Dalton was one of my table-guests. He loved to be the centre of attraction. If he wasn't, he would try to capture it with his booming asides, sometimes behaving rather like a spoilt child. I also had the good fortune to have Lord Tedder, Marshal of the Royal Air Force and Deputy Supreme Commander of the Allied Forces during the war, among my guests. Naturally *he* attracted a good deal of attention from other guests, particularly as he had been noted by Mr. Churchill, who was then Prime Minister, and they had indulged in some conversation before joining the table. This did not please Mr. Dalton, who repeatedly raised his voice to get in on the scene. Failing to achieve this, he snorted loudly, turned away and later stalked out without so much as a goodbye. But he had already repaid me my good turn when he became Minister of Local Government and Planning in 1951.

His Parliamentary Secretary rang me one Friday morning to say that the Minister would like to see me that afternoon at 4 p.m. in his office opposite the Cenotaph in Whitehall. I drove across from the house and parked my car, that Triumph Gloria, with the hood down, about thirty yards from the entrance. As I mounted the stops there was a loud, "Hello," from behind. It was Dalton, stepping out of the Ministry car. I waited on the steps, expecting to be taken into the office. Instead, he whipped out a piece of paper from his file and "confidentially" declared, with an amazing bonhommie, "Got a top-secret snippet for you. Lobby terms. I shall be opening a Welsh Office of the Ministry in Cardiff next week . . ."

Since there had been a great deal of campaigning for greater administrative facilities in Wales, this was a good scoop for me. I was pleased and went back to my car. I was giving my friend, Guy Eden of the *Daily Express*, a lift back to Fleet Street and he was seated in the front passenger seat. As I eased myself into the car, Guy grinned and said, "Not a bad story for you." Although he had been quite thirty yards away and with Whitehall traffic passing he had heard almost every word spoken by Dalton. That was the carrying capacity of the Dalton voice!

Recollections of this sort inevitably trigger off a series of other related memories. As, for instance, when I was faced with a real threat of being reported to the House for Breach of Privilege myself.

What strange threads are woven into the fabric which makes up the day-to-day operations in the House of Commons, and which involves the activities of our elected Members and those who, from the Press Gallery or the Lobby, report on them. One day relationships can be amicable and all-pervading and the next they can be soured by something like misreporting, or a revelation which upsets a particular Member, or a committee, or a group.

It happened that, one evening, I was given a piece of inform- ation which one M.P. considered, in various interests, (includ- ing his own, I subsequently discovered), should be made public. As is the way with these things, the information had been omitted by the spokesman for the Welsh Labour Group, whether deliberately or by oversight matters not. But because of that it seemed to be of special interest. The Group had been discussing the threatened closures of the East Moors Steel- works, Cardiff, and the Ebbw Vale Works. These were very important issues affecting the jobs of several thousands.

The meeting went on for quite a while and afterwards a state- ment by the Secretary, Tudor Watkins, indicated that the dis- cussion would have to be continued at another meeting. I ass- umed the reason to be that not all of the M.P.'s had had the opportunity of speaking (it had been a very well-attended meeting). I wrote my report on that basis, but shortly afterwards a telephone-call from one of those who had been present suggested an entirely different reason. We met and I was informed that the meeting had been inconclusive because of the absence of the two key figures, Jim Callaghan, in whose constituency East Moors was, and Michael Foot, M.P. for Ebbw Vale. That put an entirely different complexion on the story, especially as I was also told that both of them had been attending to personal business rather than to their constit- uency interests.

They had been, in fact, at a meeting of the Labour Party National Executive, of which both were members, in Transport House. Because it was felt that both M.P.'s should be involved in the Group's discussion and decision, the meeting had been adjourned. Furthermore, there had been some sharp criticism of their absence. Not a word of this had been included in the Secretary's statement. Naturally I wanted to know more, and I calculated that their constituents, too, would like to know why their interests had not been properly represented at this vital meeting. I was satisfied that my latest information was sound, though I suspected my informant had an axe to grind with one or both of his colleagues!

My story appeared the following morning along the lines of my information and it caused a furore in both constituencies. In no time the telephone lines to Westminster were sizzling. So were my ears from about eleven a.m. onwards. A very angry Michael Foot demanded to know where my information had come from, and demanded an immediate retraction of my story. Unless this assurance was forthcoming my offending paragraph which, he claimed, reflected him and Jim Callaghan in bad light in their respective constituencies, would be raised by him in the House. What I had written, he said, made them appear to their constituency organisations as uncaring and irresponsible. Unless the retraction was promised, he was going to raise the matter with Mr. Speaker that afternoon as a Breach of Privilege.

I had been long enough in my job by now to know that there was no Breach of Privilege, but the threat of bringing the possibility before the House gave me a sinking feeling. I didn't at that moment realise that such a step could only further publicise their situation. I determined, however, that in accordance with the Lobby code, I would not reveal the source of the information. Up to this time I had not heard from Jim. It may have been that his duties as Shadow Foreign Secretary were keeping him from the House. Michael's anger and his threat to take immediate action with Mr. Speaker had to be dealt with.

I turned to my closest personal friend in the House for advice. George Thomas, who in a few years would be occupying the Chair, was, as ever, quick to respond to my call. As a former Minister, he was fortunate enough to have a room in the Star Chamber Court Annexe. He was also on good terms with Michael Foot. Through his intervention an after-lunch meeting was arranged with Michael. Also invited to help straighten things out was Cledwyn Hughes. It duly took place in George's room and at times it proved to be pretty hot. Michael insisted on knowing who had passed on the information, but at the same time refused to confirm its truth. I refused to name my informant and asked to be told whether both of them, having had prior notice of the Group meeting, had not put the N.E.C. first without even notifying the Group they would not be attending. George sided with me in my refusal to name names and sought to pour oil on troubled waters with a compromise that I should write Michael a note expressing regret that I had not included in my story the explanation both men had given about their absence; that their presence at the N.E.C. had been essential in the Party's interest and that I understood their views on East Moors and Ebbw Vale had been conveyed to the Group.

The note would be shown by Michael at the forthcoming meeting with his constituency Management Committee and, George commented, that would serve the purpose better than any Breach of Privilege motion before the House. I agreed, but refused Cledwyn's suggestion that Michael might like to draft the note. I left the three M.P.'s in the room and returned to the Gallery, where I wrote the placatory note which ten minutes later I handed to Michael.

But what about Jim? The grapevine in the House is an extremely efficient instrument. Later that afternoon, with the threat of Privilege removed, I received a call from Jim Callaghan. Quite tersely he asked, ''Can I have from you a similar note to that given to Michael?'' Of course he could. I had kept a copy for future reference, just in case. Within minutes I was handing one over to Jim in his room just down the corridor from George's room, and we talked for a few minutes about the latest event in the foreign field and what was happening in Cardiff. No rancour and no pressurising about, ''Who told you?'' Just an acceptance that this happened from time to time when correspondents are fed with an odd piece of information. I've often wondered what happened to their notes. Perhaps they are still in the files. Mine is.

I kept my word that my informant would not be named, and I do not intend divulging it now; but the particular Member is still in the House, and he will know.

Chapter 9: A Voice for Wales

Since the turn of the century Wales, the Welsh, and the language have been prominent in the backdrop of the Parliamentary and political scenes at Westminster. Their contribution overall has been considerable, particularly with the growth of the representation of the Labour party which began with the election of Keir Hardie as M.P. for Merthyr.

It has been claimed that, at any time during a Parliament, more than a hundred of the M.P.'s—that is about a fifth of the House—are Welsh, have Welsh backgrounds, or have a direct connection with the Principality. During my time there has been justification for this claim according to such stalwarts as the late Dai Grenfell, a former Father of the House, and the Labour Old Guard veteran, the late Rt. Hon. James Griffiths.

Another who supported that contention was the self-professed historian on such matters as ''minority representation in Parliament'', the late Emrys Hughes who, despite his many years as M.P. for South Ayrshire, still spoke with the strong Welsh accent of the mining valleys of South Wales from which he had come.

Per capita, that places the Welsh in a formidable position and it is something which evokes great pride among the Westminster Welsh and which has given rise to what is known as ''The Taffia''. No one in the corridors of power doubts its force and influence when the occasion demands that ''the family'' gets together. It has even been known to cross party lines!

Wales has always been noted for the outstanding contributions of its exported talents. Preachers, teachers, lawyers, doctors, all eminent in their particular fields must, however, give way to the force of the political tributaries from the Principality which, over the years, have fed the main-stream of British politics and Parliament.

Welsh affairs have come more into their own at Westminster since the war and I am thankful that I have been in some small way party to, and witness of, this advance. I entered the House of Commons in the year of the first annual Welsh Debate, a "concession" granted by the then Leader of the House of Commons, Herbert Morrison.

There had been considerable pressure from within the Labour Party over a long period between the wars for parity with Scotland in the allocation of time and facilities for debating matters of Welsh interest. The Scottish Members had their own Grand Committee and also a number of days in each session when Scottish affairs were debated on the Floor of the House. Wales, on the other hand, had always been bracketed with England in general debates in the House and had no separate forum such as a Welsh Grand Committee. Consequently, with the return of a Labour government after the war, and with the inclusion of a number of Welshmen, it was only natural that pressures from within were mounted on Clem Attlee and the Cabinet to recognise the Welsh claim. Foremost among those claiming this recognition was Llanelli M.P., Jim Griffiths, who was also in the government. The demand was further strengthened by support from the Welsh Parliamentary Party, an influential group consisting of Welsh M.P.'s of all parties. These called for a symbolic acceptance of Welsh rights at Westminster. From the Welsh Labour Group there was an insistence that Wales should have a voice on the Floor of the House.

An odd-man-out among his Welsh Labour colleagues on this issue was Nye Bevan. It did not mean that he was less Welsh than his colleagues in the Group, but Nye, already a main force in the new government, felt there were other priorities which demanded most of his time and energy. Not least among these, of course, was the development of a National Health Service and the implementation of the Beveridge Report.

Long before it came into power in 1945 the Labour Party had promised it would consider the special position of Wales. In the aftermath of war havoc, however, the wheels were turning very slowly in that direction. It was in redemption of that early assurance of a fuller consideration of Welsh affairs in the debating chamber, open to full public scrutiny, that Herbert Morrison agreed to an annual Welsh Day. This was to be a once-a-year discussion of "matters appertaining to Wales on the Floor of the House and with a Minister to wind up where issues concerning any government department and Ministerial responsibilities were raised".

It was a giant step forward for Wales. Regrettably, however, in my judgement, Welsh M.P.'s failed to take the fullest advantage of this hard-won occasion. Instead of the explosive repercussions which might have been expected from the early debates on controversial issues (and there were many that could have been raised), Welsh Day had less effect than a damp squib. Admittedly the majority of the Welsh M.P.'s then were Labour supporters, but this should not have prevented them from having the occasional bash when matters other than the sacred cow of "constituency demands" were thought not to be receiving the required government attention. In truth, the Welsh Day forum was not exploited as it might have been, not even by the Opposition M.P.'s of Conservative and Liberal convictions.

From the start, Welsh Day became a parochial occasion on which individual M.P.'s chose to air grievances (or hail government achievements) mainly within their own constituencies. It developed more into an opportunity for self-advertisement, and there were times when I thought I knew why Nye Bevan had virtually shrugged aside any involvement in setting up a special Welsh Debate.

There was little of a national flavour or consequence about the early ones. The biggest struggles on the floor of the House were between Labour M.P.'s vying with each other to "catch the Speaker's eye" to speak their once-a-year glory piece for constituency consumption. Rarely could the M.P.'s be regarded as a united front pressing the government of the day on any particular Welsh national issue. As one who had fully supported the Morrison concession and listened to various M.P.'s promises to raise certain government shortcomings relating to Wales during forthcoming Welsh Days, I despaired of the first of those Welsh debates. I had seen more fire and fervour in local council meetings.

So-called "attacks" from the Welsh Parliamentary Party and the Labour Group were as effective as powder-puffs directed at an elephant's backside. In fact, Welsh Day on those early performances could well have been relegated to an even lower order in the Commons calendar. It might have suffered the same sad end as the Welsh Parliamentary Party, had not the 1951 General Election returned a Conservative government. This presented the Labour Group with a new and worthwhile target, which they attacked with gusto on occasions.

Even so there was little improvement and the occasion continued its parochiality until the memorable attack by David Llewellyn, the Member for Cardiff North, who blasted the B.B.C. for its alleged Welsh-language bias. It was as if a time-bomb had been thrown into the Chamber and the explosion reverberated for days and weeks to come. From that time on, Welsh Day came into its own and has remained established more as a debating and hard-hitting affair than the namby-pamby local appreciation society it threatened to be in its earliest days.

Labour's massive victory in the 1945 General Election had resulted in a dramatic change in the constitution of the two bodies which looked after Welsh affairs off the Floor of the House. Of these, the Welsh Parliamentary Party had been the more prominent. An all-party group to which every Welsh M.P. belonged, it had been dominated between the wars by the Liberals. With the Labour landside began a dramatic change which, over the years, became so pronounced that nowadays the Welsh Parliamentary Party, though officially still in existence, is virtually moribund. Its officers are still elected annually, but its meetings, which used to take place at least once a week, have lapsed. In its place the active Welsh Labour Group took over and even today constitutes the main channel of communication on issues affecting Wales in the general run of parliamentary affairs.

With the increase in the number of Conservative M.P.'s in Welsh constituencies over the past decade, a Welsh Conservative Group has been formed, but it hasn't been able to make much impact in backbench relationships with government or Ministerial departments.

When I began my work at Westminster, the Welsh Parliamentary Party met every Wednesday. It had a membership of thirty-five M.P.'s drawn from all the main parties. Its discussions cut across party lines and representations from it to governments on questions of policies relating to Wales, or matters of general Welsh public interest, or complaints, were recognised officially and always brought a response. When Liberal representation in the Commons was decimated in the 1951 general election it left Labour with an even greater overall majority and there was a marked shift of power and representation to the Labour Group.

Tudor Watkins, M.P. for Brecon and Radnor, (later Lord Watkins of Aberhonddu) was the Honorary Secretary of both the Welsh Parliamentary Party and the Welsh Labour Group. He was the longest-serving official of either body and under his astute and hard working-direction, which unashamedly reflected his Labour party affiliation, the Labour Group gradually took over. Its meetings were regular and well attended. Its activities became more and more connected with bodies in Wales which were closely associated with the Labour party, for instance local trades unions, local authorities, and Trade and Labour Councils, Chambers of Trade and the like. Only occasionally was the Welsh Parliamentary Party brought into the picture until, towards the end of the two Wilson governments, in 1969, only the Welsh Labour Group remained active.

Several attempts were made about that time by other than Labour M.P.'s to resurrect the Welsh Parliamentary body and I called repeatedly in the *Western Mail* for it to be restored. It had been a powerful instrument in the past and had served Wales well.

The Conservatives were becoming a stronger force in Wales and though still much the minority, they could have insisted on reactivating the body of which David Lloyd George, as M.P. for Caernarvon, and even during his Premiership and afterwards, right through the 'thirties, had been the most prominent advocate. All to no avail! I still feel, as I did then, that it was a great shame the Welsh Parliamentary Party should have been excluded from the conduct of Welsh affairs at Westminster, especially since a Welsh Office and Secretary of State had been created.

I am sure that I am not alone in the House in thinking that there is still a part the Welsh Parliamentary Party can play in the day-to-day conduct of public and parliamentary relation-ships even with the emergence of such parliamentary bodies as the Select Committee for Wales and the Welsh Grand Commit-tee. As official House of Commons bodies, both these are more involved with governmental and political issues. The Labour Group and the W.P.P., on the other hand, can still be useful channels through which regional and local issues and matters of complaint could be dealt with in the way originally intended, joint watchdog committees between backbench M.P.'s and their constituents where public issues are involved. This is how the Labour Group still functions, but non-Labour M.P.'s do not become involved as the united force they could be if both bodies were again operating on general, not party, lines.

The establishment of the Welsh Grand Committee in 1958 was the outcome of sustained pressures through the Welsh Labour Group upon the post-war Conservative governments. Mr. Attlee's Labour governments between 1945 and 1951 had not produced the expected Secretary of State for Wales and

Welsh Office. The Conservatives had undertaken to give Wales a greater say in the administration of Welsh affairs at Westminster, but not to the extent yet of a Secretary of State. Winston Churchill agreed to the bracketing of Welsh affairs with the Home Office as a first step and, in 1951, Sir David Maxwell Fyfe, Home Secretary, who later became Viscount Kilmuir, the Lord Chancellor, was given an additional responsibility for Welsh Affairs. It was a move which, though criticised by Labour M.P.'s as a wishy-washy compromise, nevertheless proved acceptable to Wales largely because of Sir David's popularity.

He received the accolade from the people of Wales of a nickname. He was ''Dai Bananas''—because of the ''Fyfe'' connection with the company which conducted its banana trade through Barry Docks—and he was extremely proud of it.

In connection with the appointment I recall one Sunday afternoon receiving a telephone call which gave me the first clue that the new Welsh set-up in Whitehall had been agreed by the Cabinet. David Llewellyn, who had been the M.P. for Cardiff North for only a year, told me he had only just been invited by Prime Minister Churchill to be the first Under-Secretary for Welsh Affairs under Sir David, who was Secretary of State for Home Affairs with a special portfolio as Minister for Welsh Affairs. Should he accept? His hesitancy was due to the fact that he could not speak Welsh. He thought Churchill would want one of the team to be Welsh and Welsh-speaking. He fulfilled the first consideration all right, but was an English-speaker.

It was not uncommon in those days for M.P.'s to confide in and seek the advice of their Lobby Correspondent, safe in the knowledge that, unless he had been released from a confidence, nothing would be revealed about the exchange. I had no hesitation in telling David that it was an opportunity not to be turned down . . . especially as it was an invitation from Churchill! But, he persisted, how could he get away with the fact that he was not Welsh-speaking, indeed knew only a few common-place phrases? My advice was that he should learn, and learn fast.

He accepted the post and, at the Home Office a week later, when he invited me over to see him at his desk, he thanked me and said he was learning Welsh with the aid of Welsh-language gramophone records. I did not know at the time that there was another problem which was making the decision to accept the post difficult for him. David had been warned he was suffering from a persistent illness and, as he revealed much later, he feared this would not permit him to carry out his duties effic-iently. A year later he resigned the post on the grounds of ill-health.

Because of the confidence given on Lobby terms I never mentioned that Sunday telephone conversation, but I was given permission to reveal, in a "London Letter" paragraph a week later, that the new Under-Secretary was improving his Welsh-language knowledge. Still, I had had exclusive inform-ation on the Welsh Ministers' appointments hours before a Downing Street communiqué announcing government appointments. That was the value of the Lobby system.

Although the appointment of a Minister for Welsh Affairs, albeit a secondary portfolio of the Home Office, had placated some of the more stentorian demands from the Principality for better recognition of Welsh affairs, the call for parity with Scotland continued unabated. Sir David Maxwell Fyfe surren-dered the job and moved to become Lord Kilmuir, the Lord Chancellor, with the promise of another forum at Westminster for Welsh affairs unresolved. His successor to the Welsh port-folio in 1957, Henry Brooke (later Lord Brooke) has been claimed as the one who conceived the Welsh Grand Commit-tee. Not so. He introduced the Committee, but he was not its architect.

Labour M.P.s had long discussed the possibility of a Parliamentary body whose exclusive function would be the discussion of Welsh affairs. The Attlee government, with its plethora of pro-Welsh activities, had been too preoccupied with the struggle to overcome the almost paralysing effects of war on the nation's economic and social well-being to take aboard any furtherance of Welsh administrative aspirations. After Labour's defeat in 1951, the Welsh Labour Group took up the campaign for a bigger and better say for Wales in the House of Commons, and in Opposition they were much more effective than had been the case during the six years of Labour government. A small committee was set up within the Group to advance the claim and it maintained the strictest security about its work. I was unable to penetrate this, so tight was the rule against any "leaks". However, one day in 1952 I was approached in the Members' Lobby by Ness Edwards, then M.P. for Caerphilly and formerly Postmaster General. He mentioned the idea of a Welsh Committee and took me to his room (a privilege extended to ex-Ministers in an overcrowded House of Commons) where I was shown a blue-print of what he described as "The Welsh Grand Committee". The Group had already taken up again the slogan of parity with Scotland. Ness claimed it as *his* plan, and he subsequently presented it to the Commons Select Committee on Procedure, which accepted the proposal in principle. There were reservations, however. If set up, the new committee would be unlikely to be granted the legislative powers enjoyed by the Scottish Grand Committee.

My first story linking Ness Edwards with the proposal caused a furore at Westminster, where M.P.'s claimed it had been exposed prematurely. I came under severe pressure to reveal the source of the information, but I refused to do so, with full Lobby backing. Ness never withdrew the basis of confidence under which he had given me the story and this is the first time the source has been revealed. No one was more bitter and aggressive towards me than Goronwy Roberts, M.P. for Caernarvon, who later held high offices in the Wilson governments and who became Lord Goronwy Roberts. It was not so much that the plan had been leaked; it seemed I had given the kudos to the wrong person.

Goronwy had always shown himself to be meticulous in his conduct with the Press. Not from him loose hints or gossip to project a favourable image for the Member for Caernarvon. In fact, as I recall, he had one annoying characteristic which rubbed me, and others, up the wrong way. He always adopted an upper form schoolmasterish attitude (he had, of course, been a University lecturer before being elected M.P. for Caernarvon in 1945) when communicating with us in the Lobby. He used to "dictate" his information, something I and my colleagues resented. Naturally, when our pieces appeared he would complain that it was not what he had passed on, but I don't ever remember him complaining that he had been misreported or misrepresented. On this occasion, however, Goronwy persisted in demanding to get the record straight. Quite out of character, he one day produced the "Goronwy Roberts Memorandum on the Proposal to set up a Welsh Grand Committee" which he had submitted to the Welsh Labour Group and which had been taken under the Ness Edwards wing. I still have that original memorandum. It is dated 30th April, 1952, and was the basis on which the Welsh Grand Committee was eventually set up six year later.

At first, Labour M.P.'s wanted nothing less than the same legislative powers as the Scottish Grand Committee, but, as Goronwy Roberts pointed out, that was impossible. The Scots had been able to deal with their own "domestic" legislation on Second Readings since 1948. Wales, on the other hand, had no basis of separate legislation. All Bills before Parliament were England-*and*-Wales measures. Therefore no analogy could be drawn between the Scottish and the proposed Welsh Grand Committee.

Wales had no separate legal system distinct from that of England, as Scotland had, and United Kingdom legislation had almost invariably been considered adequate to meet the needs of Wales. The Memorandum cited only three examples of specifically Welsh Bills: the Disestablishment of the Church in 1912 and in 1921, and the Intermediate Education Act of 1893. It pointed out that, in such circumstances, the Principality could hardly claim parity with Scotland in the matter of a Grand Committee. Where it *would* be possible to seek a greater Welsh standing, it was pointed out, would be if the Welsh Estimates, that is the separate expenditure on Wales out of the Exchequer, were to be published separately from those of England as were the Scottish ones. They could then be debated by the Welsh M.P.'s in committee.

To strengthen the Committee's standing it was further suggested that separate White Papers on Welsh education and industry might also be prepared for consideration by a Welsh Grand Committee. The Memorandum, therefore, proposed "that a Welsh Grand Committee be formed of the Members of Parliament for Wales and Monmouthshire to discuss the Estimates, under the chairmanship of the regular panel, the department concerned being represented by a Minister".

I tried to put the record straight with a follow-up report in the *Western Mail*. From that day onwards my relationship with Goronwy was always friendly and frank. We became and remained good friends to the end.

It was under the aegis of Henry Brooke as Minister for Welsh Affairs that the Welsh Grand Committee was established, but not in the form, or with the functions, set out in the Roberts Memorandum. In his evidence to the Commons Select Committee on Procedure, Ness Edwards had recommended that the government's annual Welsh White Paper and the Welsh Digest of Statistics should be discussed in a Welsh Standing Committee which would meet for six mornings in each Parliamentary session; and furthermore that it might be possible to remove

Rt. Hon. Henry Brooke, M.P.

the discussion of Welsh affairs from the Floor of the House of Commons altogether. That would mean giving up the annual Welsh Day and transferring this general debate to the confines of an all-Welsh M.P.'s body. The proposal was strongly opposed by Welsh Members.

Then in stepped Cledwyn Hughes (later Lord Cledwyn, Labour leader in the House of Lords) to point out, in a special report in May 1959, just before the Welsh Grand proposition was accepted by the government, that it would be possible for such a committee to conduct effective and rewarding debates upon the activities of different government departments relating specifically to Wales. He warned against giving up the annual Welsh Day, pointing out the status of such a debate compared with a debate in committee. Little did Cledwyn

'Cledwyn' (Lord Cledwyn—as Mr Cledwyn Hughes, M.P.)

realise at the time that, in a few years, he would be in the role of
poacher-turned-gamekeeper, standing at the Despatch Box as
Secretary of State for Wales, defending his government and
Office from the combined criticism of all sides of the House—
mainly on constituency issues—and in the same role, but more
vulnerable, in the Welsh Grand Committee.

In the run-up to Henry Brooke's acceptance of the Welsh
Grand Committee in 1959, it became evident that he was not
prepared to accept the package as proposed. The Memorandum
had asked for six meetings of the committee in each session. It
also required that it should be representative of all Welsh
M.P.'s, and that it would report to the Minister for Welsh

Affairs, with the rider that its deliberations and recommendations be conveyed to the appropriate authorities (that is the
departments involved in the Committee's deliberations). With
a few subtle changes, what was put on the table was a set-up
consisting of Welsh M.P.'s in committee being able to examine
in public matters relating to Wales, but without any powers of
any description. It was nothing more than another forum to add
to the conglomeration of committees which have been claimed
to be so dear to the hearts of the Welsh: a watchdog without
teeth! Mr. Brooke had accepted the demand from the Labour
M.P.'s virtually intact, but before it was implemented there
was one important change. The Committee would sit on four,
not six, mornings in each session.

Whilst the wrangle over this change was carrying on, yet
another change was being effected by the Minister. His attention had been called to the imbalance of the political parties if,
as had been proposed and accepted, the Committee should
consist only of Welsh M.P.'s. The situation at that time was
that, with the Conservatives in government, they were greatly
in the minority so far as the Welsh constituencies were concerned. This meant the government of the day could not
command a majority on the committee in the event of a vote.
Historically this had been the situation for the Tories since the
inter-war years and it could be one for the foreseeable future, so
far as Henry Brooke was concerned.

It was decided, therefore, that the Committee could only be
created on the basis of a fair representation of the state of the
Parties on the Floor of the House. This also was in accordance
with the rules of the House governing all official Parliamentary
committees. A Conservative government, therefore, would
have to co-opt its members from Tory M.P.'s with constituencies outside Wales. That ''outsiders'' should be involved in
Welsh affairs raised strong objections from Opposition M.P.'s.
But the reality at the time was that this proposal had to be
accepted or the Committee might never get off the ground. The

Minister made it more palatable to the critics by promising that the co-opted M.P.'s would be Welsh or have special Welsh interests or connections. And the government had an ample reservoir from which to draw! This compromise between the party leaders settled the issue, and this has been the basis on which the Welsh Grand has functioned since. With Conservative representation in Wales having increased, the weighting has become less of a problem for the Tories, but fluctuations with each General Election will continue to be reflected in the Committee's makeup.

Despite early forebodings, the Grand Committee has proved its usefulness . . . but it still has no teeth insofar as legislative powers are concerned. It cannot demand action in the same way as a Select Committee can. Nonetheless it is a forum which the Welsh M.P.'s of all parties would do well to preserve and make the fullest use of as an additional Welsh voice at Westminster.

There have always, of course, been those who have wished for even greater powers for Wales. In the context of a growing agitation for Home Rule, long a bone of contention within and outside Parliamentary movements, the immediate post-war years at Westminster saw definite signs of a resurrection which was gathering a more significant support from within the Welsh Labour Group than had hitherto been the case. Before the end of the first Attlee government in 1950, when it was obvious that neither government nor parliamentary time would allow for any meaningful inroads into the issue (always a political hot potato) a splinter-group of Welsh M.P.'s openly declared themselves for a measure of Home Rule. It became another thorn in the flesh of the Welsh Labour Party and more than once threatened to fester into a breakaway movement.

At that time there were twenty-seven Labour M.P.'s out of the total of thirty-six Welsh Members. Led by Goronwy Roberts (later Lord Goronwy), the Member for Caernarvon, the group comprised six Labour M.P.'s who obstinately raised their flag for Home Rule for Wales. In 1951 they were joined by the new M.P. for Anglesey, Cledwyn Hughes (now Lord Cledwyn), who had defeated Lady Megan Lloyd George (Liberal) in that General Election. It was ironic that, with that defeat, after she had represented Anglescy continuously from May 1929, Lady Megan, who had always supported the Parliament-for-Wales movement, broke with the Liberals and joined the Labour Party. She returned to Parliament in 1957 as the Labour M.P. for Carmarthen, but by then she was too late to add her name to the "rebel" movement. It had petered out, largely, I feel, because the Home Rulers within the Labour Group had overcome their fear of a growing Plaid Cymru threat within their constituencies and also owing to heavy pressures from the Welsh Labour Party for ultimate sanctions against dissident groups.

From time to time there had been attempts from the Welsh Liberals to promote Home Rule measures, and one by the young Conservative M.P. for Barry, Raymond (now Sir Raymond) Gower. This latter was not by any means a serious effort. As a Private Member's Bill which could not have won the support of his Party anyway, it was just a parliamentary ploy for throwing a spanner into the Home Rule works. About that time, in 1954, the Welsh Labour Party declared its support for a Ten-Point Plan for Wales.

This had been launched with a flourish and included a pledge for Constitutional reforms, but these fell short of a Welsh Parliament. It proposed there should be a Minister for Welsh Affairs with a seat in the Cabinet, more parliamentary time at Westminster for the consideration of Welsh affairs, and further measures of devolution. There were to be another ten years before any of these could be implemented, and finally bound up in the establishment of a Secretary of State and a full Secretariat. But the launching of the plan had the desired effect of removing a threatened division of substance within the ranks of the Labour party.

Establishment of the Welsh Office (left to right: Mr Goronwy Roberts, Minister of State; Mr J. Wiggins, Editor, *South Wales Echo*; Mr James Griffiths, Secretary of State for Wales; the Author; Mr Harold Finch, Parliamentary Under-Secretary).

The first threat to the unity of the Welsh Labour movement over Home Rule came with the formation of the splinter-group of M.P.'s whose views on this issue were in accord with the Undeb Cymru Fydd (New Wales Union) which had launched a demand for a separate Parliament early in 1950. It had immediately received the backing of Plaid Cymru. The Welsh Council of Labour, governing body of the Labour Party in Wales, refused to participate and the Parliamentary splinter-group of six "rebels" was the backlash. They held their own private meetings at the House from time to time and I was fed reports by their secretary, Tudor Watkins, M.P. for Brecon and Radnor.

It was after one of these reports that Rhys Hopkin Morris, then Liberal M.P. for Carmarthen and later Deputy Speaker, talked to me about the matter. It was his belief that the whole thing would "fizzle out", but he himself held strong personal views that Wales *should* be granted Home Rule. In fact, he tabled a Home Rule for Wales Bill which fell by the wayside for lack of parliamentary time to discuss it.

History proved him right, at least for the following forty years. In 1979 the Welsh people rejected, by a massive four-to-one majority, the government's referendum offering a form of Home Rule by way of an Elected Welsh Assembly. This was the outcome of the Wilson devolution proposals which was inherited by the Callaghan government and which was largely instrumental in ending Jim Callaghan's régime. It also ensured that no further attempt at devolution would be made for at least another ten years.

Welsh may be the oldest of our languages but it is not acceptable in the House of Commons. English, Latin where it applies
to official instruments of either House, and Norman French,
which is still used in the House of Lords to signify the Sovereign's assent to Acts of Parliament, are. Nonetheless, Welsh
has been, and still is, very much in evidence in the Palace of
Westminster. That is only natural, I suppose, when so many
Welsh men and women are in contact within its precincts.

There is a common belief that the Welsh language has little
or no commercial value. That may have been so, but believe me
it has a niche of its own at Westminster, and especially in and
about the Commons' corridors. And it *has* a value, too, as I can
well testify.

As a Welsh-speaking Lobby Correspondent I have found its
application throughout the years has brought many rewards. In
addition to cementing a closer relationship with various contacts who were Welsh-speaking themselves, there have been
occasions when a juicy morsel of information, gathered in the
Lobbies within earshot of my colleagues and non-Welsh-speak-
ing Members, has been imparted and discussed with impunity,
safe from becoming more widely known. Although knowledge
of Welsh was not a qualification required by my newspaper, it
may possibly have been felt, by those who appointed me, that it
could be an asset. If so, then they have been proved correct.

My first hint that it could sometimes give me a valuable edge
over my colleagues came from my London Editor, Edward
James. On one of his visits to the House in my earliest days
there, when he enjoyed renewal of his old contacts and a chat in
old familiar surroundings, he told me how *he* had scooped Fleet
Street by using Welsh.

It happened towards the end of the General Strike in 1926. The
Cabinet had been in session, discussing the terms of a possible
agreement with the unions. Other leading political figures had

been called in and it had been a long and wearisome wait for the journalists who had been virtually picketing No. 10 Downing Street. Suddenly there was movement. The door opened and out trooped grim-faced Ministers and others, among them the Liberal leader, David Lloyd George. Caught in the surge of his fellow reporters, Eddie James failed to elbow his way through. None of those emerging was offering anything to the clamour of the tired and irate pressmen, so, shouting above the hubbub and raising his arm, he called out, ''A oes heddwch?'' L. G. heard it. Without a flicker of recognition, though the two men were close friends, L. G. gave the traditional Gorsedd response, ''Heddwch.'' For the uninitiated it might have been merely a salutation. In fact, it had been a brilliant inspiration and the response of the politician to a long and tried confidence and friendship with the Lobby Correspondent gave Eddie James the clue to the outcome of the Cabinet decision.

''Is there peace?'' had been his shout. ''Peace,'' was L. G.'s rejoinder. It had been delivered in the presence of scores of newspapermen from all parts of the world and yet not one of them had grasped the significance. ''I left Downing Street as casually as I could, not to arouse any suspicions, and made for the nearest telephone,'' he recalled. The *Western Mail* had the peace story well ahead of any other newspaper because it had been agreed at the Downing Street meeting that no communiqué would be issued until all the unions had been notified and the agreement ratified. This must have been the most blatant and undetected Cabinet leak of all time, but there are many other instances where Welsh proved to be of inestimable value in the incessant search for stories and facts along the highways and byways of national politics.

''The Taffia'' at Westminster has long been recognised as a powerful, closely-knit body, incorporating as it does not only Welsh-speaking Members and officials, but also those who have Welsh connections. It has an unwritten code of obligations as sincere and binding as that of its Italian namesake, but

without any sinister connotation. The Land of My Fathers has a
special significance for its progeny which has no parallel among
Scottish and Irish Members. My Lobby conversations with
Welsh-speaking M.P.'s were seldom conducted in English.
Speaking in Welsh seemed to give a greater freedom of expression and a closer link. It did not always please my Lobby colleagues, but that made no difference.

One particular example I recall was when Jim Griffiths was
Minister for National Insurance in the Attlee government.
There had been a lengthy Cabinet meeting which went on late
into the evening. Lobby noses started twitching when it was
noticed that no Ministers were to be seen about the House. It
seemed there was something afoot and they were deliberately
keeping away. Adding to the suspicions was a strange clampdown from other government sources on the happenings at
Downing Street. It was well after eleven o'clock, and approching the London papers' main edition time, when some Ministers eventually made an appearance. But nobody was talking.
No-one seemed to want to be seen talking to any Lobby man.
Obviously silence had been made mandatory.

Lobby Correspondents were strategically placed in all
corners and along the corridors. There was an air of expectancy
that a big story was about to break. The Cabinet had taken some
big decision . . . but what? I was in the Central Lobby when Jim
walked in, hurriedly making for his office on the far side of the
Lobby. I approached him along with Max Mason of *The Times*,
Freddie Truelove of the *Daily Despatch* and one or two others. I
got in first by hailing him in Welsh, and he paused in his tracks.

A strict rule of the Lobby is that no-one intervenes when a
colleague has buttonholed a contact. So it was that Jim and I
talked while the others stood on the fringe and awaited their
opportunity. Our conversation was almost entirely in Welsh. I
was given guidance which allowed me to write my piece, relating to some changes in the health and national insurance
structures which later on led to Nye Bevan's resignation as

Minister of Health. There was nothing precise, nor any hint about the other matters discussed by the Cabinet. Jim was not a "leaker". Excusing himself to the others, he strode away and immediately I was pressed by Max to share the story. I said there was nothing to it and this brought an astonishing outburst from a normally placid and polite chap. It was unfair, undignified, and contrary to the spirit of the Lobby that I should conduct my interview in "a foreign tongue", he complained. He would be raising the matter with the Lobby's officials and questioning the principle of using Welsh in these circumstances. I believe he did speak to the Secretary, Guy Eden, but nothing more was heard of it, or the principle.

Many years later I was again to find Welsh a key to the opening of a much coveted door.

At no time during the Churchill post-war period in the House of Commons did I find the great war-time leader an approachable person. It was most difficult, indeed almost impossible, I would say, for anyone, except his immediate coterie, to get near enough to him even to pass the time of day. It wasn't so much his gruffness. Although the country had rejected his Party after the war, he was still The Master and the object of universal respect of M.P.'s and officials. In the Tea-Room, during his infrequent visits, in the Smoke-Room, where he would most likely be found when not on the Floor of the House, or in the corridors, few ever got within arm's length of him. In the Chamber, however, he would be the cherubic personality his wide smile could portray.

It had always been my wish to talk to Mr. Churchill, who frequently passed close to me in the Members' Lobby or the Library Corridor on his way into the House. But whilst it was no problem to approach anyone else, front or backbenchers, there always seemed to be a barrier where Mr. Churchill was concerned. It was the same for all my colleagues.

My moment arrived, however, when the former Prime Minister was granted the Freedom of the Borough of Tenby.

Because of health, or for some other reason, he was not able to visit Tenby for the ceremony. He had suggested it might take place at his London home in Hyde Park Gardens. Although it was neither a political nor a parliamentary event, I was asked to report it. Having got Conservative Central Office clearance, I turned up at No. 9 Hyde Park Gardens long before the Tenby dignitaries were due. Having satisfied the duty police officer of my bona fides, I rang the bell and was shocked to find Mr. Churchill himself in the hallway, beckoning me in with his most charming smile. Obviously he was expecting his guests, so I introduced myself as the Lobby Correspondent of the *Western Mail*, expecting him to recognise me, since he must have seen me in the House many times. But he either misheard or misunderstood me, because he seized me by the hand and ushered me into the back garden, where some chairs had been arranged on the lawn.

It was like being transported to some beautiful, peaceful, luxuriantly green oasis. The noise of London's busy traffic had been completely blotted out. Only the soft tinkle of a fountain could be heard. I was terribly embarrassed and almost overcome as Mr. Churchill, beaming and in great spirits, put his arm around my shoulders and, pacing alongside me, asked, "Do you speak Welsh?"

"Of course," I said, wondering why the question, and whether I should ask him something about the Ceremony. To my amazement he went on, "Môr o gân yw Cymru i gyd,"—in a perfect accent. Still walking up and down the lawn, he explained with a grin, "I was taught that by my old friend David Lloyd George. It was in Caernarvon back in 1911 when I went to speak for him in his election." He went on, "I was very nervous. It was my first appearance before a Welsh audience. L. G. said, 'All you have to do, Winston, is to go out and speak to them in Welsh.' But I didn't know any Welsh, so, very quickly, he taught me to say, 'Môr o gân yw Cymru i gyd'."

He asked me if I knew what it meant. I said I did, but before I had the opportunity to translate, he added, "All Wales is a sea of song." That's where the magic ended! Before we could turn the moment into an interview, the deputation arrived. It was all over, but I had been able to spend a few minutes alone with the great man and but for the brief encounter in Welsh I doubt if it could have happened.

The only other occasion when I chanced to be near enough to him had been in the Members' washroom whilst the Commons were using the House of Lords before the new Commons Chamber was built.

It was during the early part of the second Attlee government, when Labour's single-figure majority was under constant harassment by the Tories. Since Lobby Correspondents are permitted the run of the House, with the few exceptions mentioned in Chapter 6, I was using the washroom when Mr. Churchill walked in with Sir Anthony Eden, then Opposition deputy-leader. To my surprise and apprehension, they took the stalls on either side of me, seemingly oblivious of a third person. They continued their conversation which, as I recall, concerned a Vote of Censure on the Government and Sir Anthony's instruction to the Chief Whip, Pat Buchan-Hepburn. There I was, a Pressman privy to confidential information, standing between the two and conscious of my predicament should I be noticed and questions raised. I stayed there much longer than I need have, but I had to make sure both had retired before I made my way out.

I did not make use of the information which had gratuitously come my way. It was top-secret and the thought of committing a Breach of Privilege was sufficient to put me right off.

Some of the more nationalistic Welsh Members in my early days in the House sought many ways of introducing Welsh into across-the-floor exchanges during debates, or on any possible occasion. Since the Chair had to rule out its use as non-Parliamentary (this was long before Mr. Speaker Thomas's time and his natural tolerance of the Welsh language at an appropriate time—after all he was the one who proclaimed to the House that Welsh was the language of Heaven!) there were several ingenious attempts to register passively the M.P.s grievances on the issue. I recall one in particular, shortly after the Commons had moved back into their rebuilt Chamber in 1951.

Sir Waldron Smithers, the Conservative Member for Orpington, and a great linguist who, it was said, could have addressed the House, had it been in order, in either ancient or modern Greek or in Latin, intervened during a debate (I believe it was on a Welsh Day) and burst into Welsh. Mr. Speaker Clifton-Brown, somewhat perplexed, allowed Sir Waldron to carry on for a few seconds, then called him to order. Immediately there was uproar on the Welsh benches and strong protests which puzzled the Speaker.

From the Press Gallery I heard what I have never heard in the House since: Sir Waldron was reciting the Lord's Prayer. There was considerable confusion as Welsh M.P.s, hardly able to conceal their enjoyment of the incident, accused Col. Clifton-Brown of rank discrimination. They pointed out that, had Sir Waldron delivered the prayer in Latin, as he was capable of doing, he could have been in order and would not have been interrupted. But the Speaker had made a firm ruling and he adhered to it.

This was another pointer to the growing sensitivity among many Welsh M.P.s and their compatriots at that time over the Welsh language issue. It was to be another fifteen years, and after many attempts to introduce Home Rule for Wales Bills, before governments recognised there was some justification in the demand for equality between the use of Welsh and English in official matters. The outcome was legislation granting bilingual treatment of all government and publicly administered affairs in the Principality, in the Court as well as in all statutory publications. It marked the end of the England/Wales treatment.

As to the Sir Waldron episode, I was told by Dai Grenfell that it was he and S. O. Davies, M.P. for Merthyr, and a few others who had put Sir Waldron up to it. They had taught him phonetically the first words . . . ''Ein Tad sydd yn y nefoedd'' . . . It was fortunate for them, perhaps, that thc Speaker had been alert enough to bring Sir Waldron to a halt. Had he gone on a few seconds longer the Hon. Member for Orpington would possibly have been floundering.

The introduction of Plaid Cymru's (Welsh Nationalist Party) first Member, Gwynfor Evans, who had won the Carmarthen by-election in July 1966, after the death of Lady Megan Lloyd George (Labour), saw another clash in the House over the use of the Welsh language. Gwynfor insisted he would not be sworn in unless it could be done in Welsh. The Speaker at that time was the Rt. Hon. Selwyn Lloyd, and the ironic thing was that he, too, was of Welsh extraction, though not Welsh-speaking.

'Gwynfor' (Mr Gwynfor Evans, first Plaid Cymru M.P.)

I recall having been tipped off by both Mr. Speaker's Office and by some Plaid supporters early that morning that there would be a unique situation when it came to Gwynfor's taking the Statutory Oath of Allegiance. So I was ready when, at the end of Question Time, with the new Member having been escorted the Clerks' Table and the Despatch Box, where the Bible on which the Oath is taken is always kept, Gwynfor stood resolutely shaking his head. Quietly and determinedly he requested that he take the oath in the Welsh language. It had never happened before!

Mr. Speaker courteously thanked Mr. Evans for having given him advance notice of the request and did what all Speakers do when faced with a new situation. He drew on precedent, or as close to precedent as the occasion would allow. The House of Commons, with its centuries of tradition, does not favour much the setting of new precedents, but obviously this one could not be avoided. "I sympathise with his desire to speak in one of the great languages of the United Kingdom, especially as both my mother and father were Welsh," said the Speaker. The House was silent as the drama unfolded, and Badge Messengers —those elegantly dressed officers of the House with their gilt Badge of Office setting off their immaculate sartorial presence —kept a watchful eye on the public galleries in case of a demonstration. Then Mr. Speaker gave his ruling.

He referred to one which had been given by "a predecessor who himself spoke fluent Gaelic . . ." He was referring to Mr. Speaker Morrison who, asked whether he would allow a speech in Welsh, had replied, " 'Except ye utter by the tongue words easy to understand, how shall it be known what is being spoken?' " They were the words of St. Paul (First Epistle to the Corinthians, Chapter 14, verse 9). M.P.s, he then ruled, had to address the House of Commons in English.

Eventually there was a compromise. Gwynfor took the Oath first in English and then in Welsh, thus himself establishing a precedent which will be available in the future to any Welsh-speaking Member of Parliament. Thus was added another chapter to the turbulent history of the Welsh language in Parliament.

Chapter 11: On and off the Air

By the mid-fifties I had become established as a regular broadcaster on Welsh regional and national political affairs. It had begun by agreement with my then Editor, David Cole, who had realised the benefit to the *Western Mail* of my being by-lined as "The *Western Mail's* Political Correspondent at the House of Commons". In those days the B.B.C. had to rely greatly on contributors where political programmes were concerned. There was nothing like the corps of parliamentary and political staff-men that exists today. So the introduction on the air was a plug for my newspaper as well as for me.

The arrangement worked very well because the Welsh B.B.C. did not have a staff-man at the House and its presenters valued the freelance services of a Lobby Correspondent at a fraction of the cost of employing a staff-man, assuming that the House authorities would allow another accreditation for the broadcasting service. There was the added attraction, I suppose, that I was fully informed on Welsh affairs in particular and had a valuable relationship with the M.P.'s Cardiff would be requiring from time to time. The one stipulation made by my editor was that the service by me would not be a news-service, since that would not be in the best interests of my paper. I too favoured this arrangement. Discussions and commentaries on topical issues involving the Houses of Parliament, either on a personal basis or with M.P.s and Peers, were all that was permitted.

It was helpful to publicise the *Western Mail*, and I also saw it a good opportunity to bring myself into public notice, since the newspaper had not up to then adopted the name by-line practice. So it happened that I became a regular broadcaster with a weekly programme entitled "Wales at Westminster" presented by Jack Richards. Following this was "Focus", also a weekly series during the parliamentary sessions.

Looking back on the copies of the scripts of those discussions with M.P.'s which later became live chat-shows from Broadcasting House in London on Friday evenings, I can realise now, more than at that time, how much they brought home to those listeners who were keen on politics. They also brought the M.P.'s closer to their constituents, and there was no dearth of applicants for a place on the programmes.

Listeners' correspondence gave testimony of their enjoyment of the programmes and the rumbustious exchanges which took place between the three participating M.P.'s, who were always representative of the main Parties in the Commons. They continued for about ten years,—indeed there seemed no reason why they should not have gone on much longer, . . . but in 1964 "Wilson's Hundred Days" scuppered them, and me.

I had been invited by the Wales and the West Television pundits to do a ten-minute piece on the first hundred days of Harold Wilson's 1964 government. In the General Election

On the air, 1962 (left to right: Geraint Morgan, M.P.; Tudor Watkins, M.P.; the Author; Emlyn Hooson, M.P.).

campaign, he had promised a hundred days of dynamic action and the television people thought it would be a good thing to review and assess the Prime Minister's achievements over that period. I went off to Bristol for the rehearsal, which was intended to be a straightforward interview with a Lobby Correspondent. There was to be nothing parochial about it. Harold Wilson was to be put to a full public examination on the reasons for the absence of any dynamism in the first period of government. The rehearsal proceeded well enough and off I went to a casual lunch. When I reported back to the studio, everything was in turmoil.

It was no longer what Harold Wilson had done in his first hundred days that was preoccupying the presenter. The emphasis had changed dramatically to what was Harold Wilson going to do about Patrick Gordon-Walker, his Foreign Secretary, who had been defeated in Smethwick during the General Election but had immediately been given the Labour ticket for a by-election in the supposedly unloseable seat of Leyton. This manoeuvre had given Wilson the means of keeping open the Foreign Office post in the almost certain knowledge that Gordon-Walker would hold the seat for Labour. But he didn't, and on that Friday lunchtime in January 1965 Whitehall was suddenly in sheer panic, and Britain was without a Foreign Secretary.

I was invited to switch the topic of the interview. To blazes with Wilson's Hundred Days! What about Wilson's immediate dilemma of finding another Foreign Secretary from a Cabinet which had only newly been formed? There I was, stranded in Bristol, and my paper wanting to know what were the political moves taking place in Whitehall. I was lucky enough to have a close friend inside No. 10 Downing Street. While the cameramen and crew were preparing for the original interview I was able to get through to Downing Street and make contact.

For a holding piece, whilst I was on my way back to London, I was told on Lobby terms that Michael Stewart was to be switched from Minister of Education to Foreign Secretary (a most improbable appointment one would have thought), and that the announcement would not be made before 6 p.m. This ruled out any chance of my waiting in Bristol for the live interview on the original programme and it was suggested that the ''canned'' take should be used. Out of sympathy for the producer, I passed on the information about the new appointment so that, should there be an enforced change in programme arrangements, and my interview be slotted in after the news headlines at 6 o'clock, they could be well prepared in advance. It was just before 3 o'clock at the time.

It was suggested, however, that my interview should be done again on film, in condensed form, with one or two slight changes. I agreed. The opening gambit was, as we had agreed, ''What dynamic action has been achieved in these first hundred days?'' I likened the operation to Napolean's retreat from Moscow. All Wilson's government had done in that time was to legislate for free local bus services for pensioners. No major issues had been tackled, as promised . . . I *had* intended giving the reason, namely that, with a majority of three, no Prime Minister *could* embark on any major controversial legislation. But the interviewer's switch to the surprise election defeat at Leyton was too quick.

I was pressed for my views on the Gordon-Walker aftermath and the new Wilson crisis, and taken much deeper into a party-political controversy than I could have anticipated. Afterwards, I had to agree that the references to the hundred days ''dynamism'' had been a gross (though not a deliberate) lampoon. Furthermore, the timing of the programme had not been changed to immediately after the News; it went out at the original time, ten minutes before 6 p.m. This had given Television Wales and the West a ten minutes' start on the official release, and I had been responsible for a Downing Street leak.

The hundred days references greatly incensed Labour M.P.'s and over the weekend there were threats of a House of Commons censure motion against me and the programme. Thankfully nobody seemed to have noticed that the embargo on the appointment notice had been broken.

I recall the Welsh Labour Group—or some of its members—demanding a broadcast apology and a retraction by me. Tudor Watkins, the Group's secretary, handed me an official complaint and for a time I thought my days in the Lobby were numbered. But there was nothing I could do, and the programme producers seemed quite indifferent. I realised no Breach of Parliamentary Privilege was involved, but Labour M.P.s were determined I should be punished. It was then I learned an invaluable lesson about the power behind the scenes of the political groups operating at Westminster, and in particular the influence held over the B.B.C. at that time. A few days later I was asked by Cardiff to meet the Wales B.B.C. Director, Alun Oldfield Davies.

We were both members of the National Liberal Club in London, and that is where we met. He showed me a letter from the Welsh Group demanding that I should not be allowed to continue broadcasting for the Welsh B.B.C. There had to be an immediate break, he told me. He could not ignore the "command", the forces were too strong. Despite my protestations, I was "struck off" and about ten years of significant broadcasting services were sunk without trace.

Officially the explanation was that the programme format was in need of a change. But what a change! . . . The gap caused by taking my series off the air was filled by the M.P.'s themselves. They requested, and got, five minutes' time on the air each week on a rota basis reflecting the respective party strengths. This resulted for the most part in nothing more than M.P.'s giving extracts from Hansard of the week's happenings, with particular reference to constituency interests. It didn't take long for Labour M.P.'s to realise, however, that since it was on the basis of one from each party consecutively, and with Labour having about two thirds of the Welsh seats, the Welsh

Tories and Liberals were getting proportionately far more time on the air, and individual Labour Members had long waits in between their turns. This "inequality" could not be tolerated and before long the format was withdrawn. I was never allowed to resume my own political chat programme which had been so successful for everyone concerned.

Chapter 12: Cardiff and the Welsh Development Corporation

It is, as I write, thirty-one years since Cardiff was declared the Capital of Wales on 20th December 1955, the culmination of many years' dour competition with Caernarvon for the honour. I had kept close to the cut-and-thrust between South and North Wales M.P.s and the arrival of Major Gwilym Lloyd George as Home Secretary and Minister for Welsh Affairs in October 1954 brought the decision much nearer. We had formed a friendly association from the time I entered Westminster, when he was the M.P. for Tenby. He had been very helpful to me in many matters of Lobby enquiries.

According to my diary, it was December 15th when his Private Office rang me to say the Minister would be happy to join me for lunch. I immediately confirmed our usual table in Rules, Maiden Lane, and, when I called back to confirm with the Private Office, I was told the Minister would pick me up in New Palace Yard immediately after Cabinet. He did and during our lunch he told me, off the record, that the Cabinet had agreed to his proposal that Cardiff should now be granted Capital status. He explained that there would be no need for a decree from Buckingham Palace or from the Home Office. All that was required was a statement to Parliament. The information was not being given to me for immediate release, it should be treated on Lobby terms. This meant that, when the appropriate question appeared on the Order Paper of the House, I could ''speculate'' as to the answer. This was in the usual Lobby way.

Over the weekend the question appeared, in the name of David Llewellyn, the Conservative M.P. for Cardiff North, for answer on Tuesday. It was, of course, an 'inspired' question as is the custom when a Minister seeks to impart some information to the House. Sitting on that information was one of my toughest ordeals at the House. I was unable to publish it because of our strict Lobby rules on confidence. What actually happened was that I took my Editor into my confidence on the Sunday, so that he could prepare for the story, and on Tuesday morning the paper was able to state that later that day it would be announced in Parliament that Cardiff was to be formally recognised as Capital of Wales.

Why it had been done in this way, I did not know, but there was considerable animosity from the North Wales M.P.'s, all of them Labour, at being faced with a *fait accompli*. Fortunately, there being no proclamation with the customary attendant celebrations to exacerbate the situation, good relations were soon restored between South and North Wales M.P.'s. Thinking back on this and similar events only brings back to me more forcibly the privilege it has been to have served in the Lobby for the past forty years. Many of the experiences which I am now relating were possibly only because I was lucky enough to be in the right place at the right time.

It was an astonishing stroke of good fortune, for instance, which enabled me to get the exclusive story of the creation of the Development Corporation for Wales, even before the ink was dry on the paper which bound the government and a number of leading Welsh industrialists to this "Help Wales" project back in 1957.

David Llewellyn had invited me to dinner one slack evening in the House. Because of the possibility of a vote, we went across the way to St. Stephen's Club, where M.P.'s entertained their guests in close proximity to the House. We had not finished when the Division Bell rang and off he went to vote, leaving me to await his return. A telephone-call told me he had been delayed, so I finished my meal alone and casually made my way through the foyer and on to the Embankment.

Standing at the entrance were Sir Julian Pode, Managing Director of the Steel Company of Wales, and Mike Wheeler, Managing Director of Guest, Keen and Nettlefolds, Cardiff. Both were old friends.

We exchanged greetings casually and Julian asked me whether I was waiting too. A strange question! I didn't ask what he meant, but said something like, "He's not coming back. He's been delayed after the vote . . ." meaning David, of course.

Mike said, "In that case, let's go on. We have a car outside. Would you like to come up with us?" Some sixth sense told me something was happening, so I agreed readily.

We were off to the Dorchester, I was informed. They express-ed surprise that I had been told about the meeting, because they were of the impression that it was being kept under wraps. My stock-in-trade reply that a secret shared between two or more people doesn't long remain a secret seemed to have the desired effect, because straight away they filled me in on the details of how the Corporation had been mooted and approved by Henry Brooke, Minister of Welsh Affairs, and Lord Brecon, his Minister of State. "Viv" Brecon had been acting as liaison-man between a group of leading industrialists and the project was now ready to be launched. And I had not heard a whisper about it!

It was necessary to tie up some of the financial ends to secure an office in New York as a base for the American outlet, hence the meeting with Henry Brooke and Lord Brecon and some others. The government, I was told, was putting up £5,000 as a first stake. Small money in government terms today, but no small amount at that time. Also it was a matter of principle, which could be challenged by other parties in the House, if it was construed that the government was granting carte-blanche to a private enterprise. The details kept coming, but I dared not bring out a notebook to record the conversation. That would have given the game away. They did not have an inkling that what I was being told I was hearing for the first time.

When we arrived at the Dorchester I was ushered into the dining-room, where a table had been reserved and was, in fact, being occupied by Sir Robert McAlpine, head of the big con-struction firm, and another industrialist from Wales whose name escapes me. I joined in another very good meal, sorry only that I had already partaken at the St. Stephen's, and continued to pick up more information whilst queasily awaiting the arrival of the two Ministers. Excusing myself for a few minutes, I telephoned my Editor, David Cole, whose go-ahead ideas and political perspicacity had ensured that political stories, according to their value in interest and effect, had a new prominence in the *Western Mail*. It was getting on for eleven o'clock and edition time. I explained the set-up and we agreed the story would have front-page lead; but I had to be certain the Ministers would go ahead with the plans. Still without showing (I hoped) the anxieties I felt, I returned to the table. Half an hour later Henry Brooke and Lord Brecon walked into the dining-room. Never shall I forget the looks on their faces as they advanced to the table which, by this time, was quite jolly.

Henry Brooke would have made a good Poker player. After the initial surprise, he made their apologies for being held up at the House and got down to the business in hand without further ado. But he sat at the farthest end of the table from *me*. Lord Brecon, on the other hand, was furious, and showed it. What the devil did I think I was playing at, he asked me in an undertone.

My answer was quite simply that I was seeking confirmation that the government was backing the Corporation project. But inside I was quaking somewhat because I feared that I would be warned against publishing anything. I believed he was about to raise the question of an injunction with his Minister and others at the meeting when I whispered, "It's already in the paper, 'Viv'." Lord Brecon, with whom I had spent many hours since he had been so romantically whisked off the terraces during a 'Varsity rugby match at Twickenham as Viv Lewis, Brecon quarry owner and industrialist, leading Welsh Conservative, and drafted into the government as Minister of State for Wales, rather reluctantly left me alone. I wandered back to the telephone to ring David Cole and confirm the story was O.K.

Both Ministers displayed considerable finesse in dealing with what, for them, must have been an acutely embarrassing situation. So much so that, when one of the group suggested that, it being one a.m. and the talks continuing, I might be taken home in his chauffeur-driven car, no one raised any objection. I was driven home in the luxury of a Rolls Royce, which gave me more satisfaction and contentment than a cat with a bowl of double cream. An added bonus was the memory of the Ministers' looks when they found me hob-nobbing with Sir Robert and the others.

Chapter 13: Dai Grenfell

The thirty-six Welsh M.P.s who made up the Principality's representation when I first arrived at Westminster undoubtedly contained those with the greatest potential of any intake. Labour were in the overwhelming majority and included Jim Callaghan and George Thomas. The former, after holding several high offices of State, was to become Prime Minister. The other, now Viscount Tonypandy, became Speaker, indeed one of the greatest in a long line of Speakers. He was, and remains, my closest, staunchest and oldest friend in the House, and there will be other references to his tenure of office and his invaluable contributions to Parliament.

Already a Member of fifteen years' standing was Nye (Aneurin) Bevan, stormy petrel of the pre- and post-war Labour Party. A brilliant orator and administrator, his genius had not reached its pinnacle when ill-health claimed him before Labour's return to power in 1964. Had he survived a few more years, history would have had to be rewritten. After Hugh Gaitskell, with whom he became closely allied not long before his death (Gaitskell himself died within a year, dealing the Labour Party a double body-blow) Nye was the one who could have united and further matured the party.

It was in the shadow of this double tragedy that Harold Wilson came from the wings to emerge in 1964 as the new leader and the second Labour Prime Minister since the war. He came to power to the clamour of "thirteen years of Tory misrule". It was his battle-cry for the 1964 General Election, and he stayed at Downing Street until 1970.

Then there was Jim Griffiths, the veteran Old Guard who steered the party through internecine troubles time and again, was its deputy leader, and finally emerged as the first Secretary of State for Wales.

Doyen of the Welsh Labour M.P.s at that time, however, was D. R. Grenfell, M.P. for the Gower, who had been a

Minister for Mines between 1940 and 1942. He was an astonishing person, a self-taught linguist of no mean repute who had
gone down the mines at the age of twelve and worked there for
twenty-three years, during which he became Miners' Agent.

We had known each other from my Bridgend days, and he was
one of the M.P.'s with whom I invariably spoke Welsh. In my
first weeks at the House of Commons it was Dai Grenfell who
"sponsored" me with introductions to other M.P.s. I cannot
say that from the very beginning these were easy associations.
There was nothing personal involved, but nary a one of the
Labour M.P.s regarded me as a persona grata. I had to *earn* my
spurs. And the reason was the newspaper I represented. The
Western Mail, in Labour's eyes, was still the coal-owners'
paper, and as such a natural enemy of Labour M.P.s, especially
those from the South and West of Wales. Once having established, however, that I was there to report fairly and without
party bias, I became one of the family. I was always treated
properly even though sometimes, I considered, unfairly
because of the taint from which my newspaper continued to
suffer.

My first major story came through Dai Grenfell, and in retrospect it was the most sorrowful one. As a new-boy I was prone to
stay a little longer in the House than was sometimes necessary.
I would be feeling my way around and meeting different M.P.s
from other areas. That is how it was on this particular Friday, a
day when the House normally managed to complete its Private
Members' business and depart before the lunch-hour.

With very few about, I was exploring the corridors leading
from the Central and Lower Waiting Room lobbies to the House
of Lords. As I turned into the Members' Dining-Room corridor I
heard someone sobbing. As I got nearer I saw it was my old
friend, Dai. To see such a mature and tough person sitting, head
bent, on a bench in the empty corridor, and sobbing heavily,
moved me very much. I thought at first he might be unwell. I
enquired what was the matter and all the bitterness he must

have been feeling was evident when he literally spat out, "It's that b . . . Jim Griffiths. I'll never speak to him again." Then came the explanation.

Dai had been working assiduously on an assurance given by Prime Minister Attlee that a new steel plant in South Wales was to be in his constituency. Dai intended to confirm to his constituency Management Committee that very night that everything had been settled. Much preparation had been done in secret and a government statement would announce the site of the new Welsh steel strip-mill as Velindre, near Swansea.

It had been arranged for Dai to meet the Minister of Supply, John Wilmot, that morning to receive the go-ahead for a local announcement. Whilst waiting outside Wilmot's office in the House, he had noticed Jim Griffiths emerging. Minutes later he was being told by the Minister there had been a last-minute change of plan. Mr Griffiths, he was told, had made out a stronger case for Llanelli on sociological and unemployment grounds, and taking into account the rundown of the tinplate industry. (Llanelli had always been regarded as "The Tinopolis"). The site, therefore, would be at Trostre. This was the story as Dai then gave it to me.

The shock, after the initial outburst of anger, had reduced him to a sobbing hulk. How was he to explain it to his Management Committee? Only a week earlier he had confided in them the firm future for the Morriston, Gorseinon and Swansea areas.

In his bitterness, as he sat there on the bench, with me a very sympathetic listener, he drew from his pockets documents which revealed, for the first time, a blue-print of the proposed mill and its development; how the government had commissioned a site survey at Llangyfelach at a cost of £80,000 (quite a large sum in those days) which had proved it to be a suitable location. There were many other details. "Take them!" said Dai, and abruptly left. I hadn't even had the chance of asking him if I could use the documents, or whether this story of intrigue and double-cross—as he had described it—could be written. I was very troubled about it.

The sequel: I returned as usual to our Fleet Street office to help with the "London Letter" column and the weekend feature, "Talk in the Clubs". We worked until close on nine o'clock when Eddie James, my London Editor, asked whether there was anything wrong. He was putting on his coat and had noticed, from my attitude throughout the evening, that something was amiss. In fact, I had been troubled by the spectre of Parliamentary Privilege if I decided to write the story and publish the papers which Dai had thrust into my hands. There was also the breach of confidence under the Lobby rules, since I had not been told to go ahead, and as a newcomer this also worried me.

I decided to put the entire facts before him . . . I can see it all now, Eddie James peeling off his coat, the piercing glare and a vituperative thirty seconds which seemed like an eternity, ending with, "Get Cardiff on the 'phone." With the confidential papers before him and with a notepad being rapidly covered with shorthand as he sketched out the story from my details, he dictated the account of Trostre, the new mill-site chosen in preference to Velindre. He omitted, however, the personal details.

I learned more that evening about parliamentary and political reporting, and how to keep within the bounds of confidence without detracting from the paper's interests, than in the whole of the next five years. Strange to relate, Dai never once mentioned the incident to me. It had passed between us without rancour. But he never forgave Jim. They never got back on speaking terms, and all their colleagues knew why.

Some recompense was forthcoming, however, but not during Dai's days in the House. The steelworks eventually came to Velindre, but it was Dai's successor, Ifor Davies, who had the pleasure of seeing it built and operating. The foundations, however, had been laid by D. R. Sadly the works as such is now no more.

Another encounter with Dai strained our relationship for a time. He had been on one of his lecture-tours of America and, as was customary among M.P.'s on these public-relations visits, he gave me a ring and suggested there might be a nice paragraph for the "London Letter" or the gossip-column. It had happened, he told me, that whilst in Pennsylvania he was invited to address a meeting with many Welsh ex-patriates present. To his astonishment, the chairman turned out to be an old miner "butty" from Fforestfach. They were both approaching their seventies, I believe.

Enthusing over the recollection, Dai went on, "He gave me a wonderful introduction at that meeting. He said how young and virile I still looked . . ." Seeing nothing wrong with it, I quoted him in the story. Next morning, on my arrival at the House, I was given a message that Mr. Grenfell wanted to see me and would be waiting in the Central Lobby. I went straight there to meet him.

I knew there was something wrong as soon as I saw him clutching a copy of the *Western Mail*. I had barely reached him before he jumped up, seething with anger. He raised the paper as if to hit me and shouted, "You dirty little b . . .! I'll give you virile." I cannot remember if there were many people about, but Dai Grenfell in a temper was a terrifying sight. And that morning he was at his worst, I think. I turned and ran, neither waiting for an explanation of the outburst nor offering any defence. What the onlookers thought, I do not know, but I ran off into the Lower Waiting Room and up the Dining-Room corridor into the Lords Lobby. So far as I knew, Dai was still chasing me. What a ridiculous sight it must have been—a young man on the run and an elderly man in hot pursuit! But with me at that moment it was a case of discretion being the better part of valour. The picture which occupied my mind as I ran was of being involved in a Breach of Parliamentary Privilege by becoming embroiled in fisticuffs with an M.P. It added to my momentum, I think. All I wanted was to get away from the angry Dai.

I kept well clear of him for the rest of the day. That evening, however, I mentioned the incident to Eddie James. "That's funny," he remarked. "*I* remember being chased by Dai Grenfell in a rage around the corridors when I was fairly new at the House. He was much younger then, of course, but he had a hell of a temper . . ." And they say lightning never strikes the same place twice!

Later I was given the reason for his outburst. It was the subeditor's treatment of the story, which appeared on the front page. The headline merely said "THE VIRILE MR. GRENFELL". Nothing wrong in that, you might suppose. Dai, however, had put the wrong connotation on "virile". And being Welsh, and at his age, he felt he might be subjected to some curious glances in his constituency . . . not all of them, perhaps, admiring!

It came out all right in the end. When the temper had subsided, and he was more relaxed, we met casually in the Members' Lobby and had a bit of a laugh after I had explained it was none of my doing. Apparently some of his colleagues on the Welsh table in the Tea-Room had suggested to him that his new lease of life might be the subject of a "full and frank" debate. So far as I could make out, nobody ever again made mention of Dai's virility. Word of our "encounter" had got around; after that, for a bit of clean fun, it was always the "agile" Dai Grenfell!

The years passed but Dai Grenfell's ill-feeling for Jim Griffiths lingered on. After D. R. had retired I discussed the vendetta more openly with Jim and found him very forthcoming. I mentioned the scene I had witnessed that fateful Friday and the story I had heard. It was then I was told that there was another side to it.

After Dai's death and Jim's retirement in 1970, I had another meeting with the former Secretary of State for Wales at his home in Putney during which we discussed the other side of the affair. He promised to put it on record and in his handwritten letter to me, which I have retained, is his authorisation for publishing his account now.

It is written in the context of post-war steel and tinplate development in Wales and particularly the creation of the Margam and Trostre strip-mills and the Velindre works. It is of considerable interest as background to the present-day situation, especially when we consider the turnaround of an industry from being a colossal money-loser into a sound viable structure.

Looking back over nearly fifty years to the emergence of the strip-mill, Jim Griffiths claims its pioneer in Wales to have been Sir William Firth. He, and a colleague, Henry Folland, had set about amalgamating some of the older works in South West Wales. By the 'thirties they had formed a combine, The Grovesend Company, and were the leading employer in the area. The story goes that Firth built up a close friendship with one of the Welshmen who had emigrated from Pontardulais to the U.S.A. He was Edgar Lewis who, by the 1930's, had become the head of one of the biggest steel and tinplate combinations in the United States, the Jones Loughlin Group. He had already built a new strip-mill for his company and its success had attracted world-wide attention. He urged Firth to build one of these new-fashioned mills in Britain and in due course Firth let it be known he intended to pioneer the new type of mill in this country.

At first the intention was warmly welcomed, but when he announced where he intended to build, it created consternation in the ranks of Welsh tinplate workers. The new mill was to be sited near to the sources of iron ore in Oxfordshire, Northamptonshire and Lincolnshire. He chose the village of Irthlingborough, Northants, for his first mill. This stirred the whole of Wales into action. Local authorities, Trades Unions, the political parties, Chambers of Commerce and even the Churches, united in a demand that the government should act to ensure that the new mill was built in South Wales. By common consent it was urged that the site should be in one of the areas of the old industry which had been most grievously affected by the Great Depression. Ebbw Vale was selected and, recalling the decision, Jim Griffiths wrote:

'Jim' Griffiths.

"The Welsh Parliamentary Party (a unique institution in the House of Commons since it brought together all the 36 Welsh M.P.s of the Welsh constituencies, irrespective of party) was called upon to intervene in the matter. I was by this time one of the Welsh M.P.s and a member of the Welsh Parliamentary Party. We held a special meeting and decided upon an unusual course. Normally the practice would be to send a deputation to see the Minster responsible for an industry, but we decided on this occasion to ask the Prime Minister to receive all the 36 Members.

"The Prime Minister at the time was Stanley Baldwin, and his family firm, Baldwin's, had been, and still was, one of the important firms in the steel and tinplate as well as the coal industries. He agreed to our request and arranged for us to see him at the Prime Minister's room in the House of Commons. With the Prime Minister was the Chancellor of the Exchequer, Neville Chamberlain. The Prime Minister opened the meeting by stating he would be glad to listen to our representations. It had already been arranged that the M.P.s of the constituencies most seriously affected should put the case. These included the Member for Ebbw Vale (Aneurin Bevan) and the Member for Llanelli (Jim Griffiths).

"Whilst Nye Bevan was speaking, David Lloyd George (still M.P. for Caernarvon Boroughs), came into the room. This was a surprise and caused the Prime Minister to interrupt the proceedings in order to express his pleasure at the visit of his old rival. The Chancellor, however, looked rather taken aback. After those selected to put the case had spoken, Lloyd George asked the P.M. if he could be allowed to say a word and he proceeded to make a fervent plea, as a Welshman, to a Baldwin with a long family association with Wales, to help save our valleys from disaster.

"The Prime Minister was obviously moved, and when he came to reply referred to his own association with the family's mills and mines in Wales. Then, turning to the Chancellor, he said—'Neville, we must see into this at once.' We thanked him and left. Soon it was announced that Firth had changed his plans and that the strip-mill would be built at Ebbw Vale. This was a triumph for Wales, and it was to lead to Wales becoming one of the important centres of the new strip-mills, and to ensure for Wales a place in the steel and tinplate industries in the years ahead.''

*   *   *

The next chapter in Jim's story brings us to the post-war periods of the 1940's and 1950's. He continued,

''The building of Ebbw Vale had been preceded by the formation by Firth of a new combine composed of the old firms which became associated in the new combination of Richard Thomas and Baldwins. The success of the new venture at Ebbw Vale led to some of the other companies in the industry joining in the formation of the Steel Company of Wales. In the immediate post-war period, from 1945 onwards, S.C.O.W., as it became more familiarly known, announced its intention to build a large integrated steel, sheet and tinplate plant based on Margam (Port Talbot) in South West Wales. The new works was to include steel furnaces, a hot roll-mill and cold reduction plants. The combined plants, it was estimated, would provide employment for from 15,000 to 20,000 workers.

''The Company's plan was to build the new combined plants on one site at Margam. It was argued by the Company that the site would be:

(1) Cheap to procure as it was mainly on sand and sand dune,

(2) That it would run alongside the main railway from South Wales to London,

(3) That it was also close to the Port Talbot Harbour and Docks which could be enlarged to provide direct unloading of imported raw materials from ship to works,

(4) That it would provide all the benefits to be derived from 'economy of size'.

''However, there was another side to the coin. The Margam plant would inevitably lead to the closures of a number of steel-works and sheet and tinplate mills in the area west of Port Tal-bot, and these included Swansea and Llanelly. The Plan, as prepared by S.C.O.W., was submitted to the government dep-artment at that time responsible for the industry—the Ministry of Supply. The Minister in the Labour government at the time (it was Clem Attlee's first Administration) was John Wilmot.

''I was serving in the government as Minister of National Insurance and in due course the papers setting out the S.C.O.W. Plan reached my desk. I realised at once the impli-cation for the area west of Port Talbot, including the town of Llanelly and its surrounding villages where it would mean the closure of many of the old works. This would be a fatal blow to the industrial future of my constituency. I sought a meeting with my colleague, John Wilmot, and learned from him that his advisers were of one mind in urging him to approve the plan. Neither Wilmot nor I were at that time members of the Cabinet, and so, in view of my concern, we agreed to seek a meeting with Sir Stafford Cripps. As President of the Board of Trade he had oversight of the activities of the Minister of Supply in the industrial field as well as for the implementation of the government's policy for the Development Areas—which, of course, included South Wales.''

It was at this point that Jim moved on to the Grenfell Affair, and in recounting what happened after he had become aware of the implications and far-reaching effects of the S.C.O.W. Plan as revealed in that memorandum which he happened to notice among other papers on his desk, Jim Griffiths gives a classic example of behind-the-scenes power-play at Westminster which can so easily affect the lives of scores of thousands of people. They become the pawns in a mighty game of political chess. The meeting with Sir Stafford having been arranged through John Wilmot, the account continues:

"At this meeting I argued that whereas the case for siting the major plants at Margam was unanswerable, yet, bearing in mind the consequences for the areas around Swansea and Llanelly, consideration should be given to siting some of the sections of the combined plants in those areas. Stafford Cripps supported my proposal and asked John Wilmot to discuss it with the Company. This he did and eventually the Company put forward a revised plan which would separate the Cold Reduction Plants from Margam, provided sites were chosen which would have direct railway connection with Margam. They later proposed that there would be two Cold Reduction Plants, at Trostre, Llanelli, and at Velindre, near Swansea.

"This new plan was discussed at a further meeting with Sir Stafford Cripps and I at once expressed my pleasure and hoped the Cabinet would approve. I also discussed the new proposals with Hugh Dalton, who had associations with the areas—his mother was a member of a Neath family. He was also interested as the author of the Development Areas Act and was in agreement with the action I had taken to seek the dispersal of part of the mammoth Margam Plant. It fitted in with his ideas of providing new industries as near as possible to the communities affected by the closure of the old industries. Dalton was M.P. for Bishop Auckland, a coal-mining area which, like South Wales, was plagued by unemployment following the depression in the coal industry.

"The Cabinet duly considered and approved the Margam/Trostre/Velindre Plan and the Company was authorised to proceed with the erection of the plants. As it was the plan the Company had submitted, my colleagues and I thought that this would now be implemented as agreed. But someone in S.C.O.W. had, it appears, opposed the proposal and submitted an alternative—for one Cold Reduction Plant to be sited at Port Talbot and the second at Velindre. When I learned about this I again took up the matter with John Wilmot and Stafford Cripps. They both expressed their concern as the new plan was contrary to the agreement made by the Company and the government. When John Wilmot took up the matter again with the Company he was told that they had already begun to prepare the foundations for the plants at Margam and Velindre, and that they were abandoning the Trostre site.

"This infuriated Stafford Cripps, who told Wilmot and me that he would propose that if only one Cold Reduction Plant was to be built outside Margan then it would have to be at Trostre. As the Company had already leaked their Margam/Velindre scheme, Stafford made a statement that the government had decided that one of the Cold Reduction Plants would have to be located, on sociological grounds, at Trostre. This gave rise to controversy with some of my colleagues whose constituencies included Swansea and the Velindre areas. In this controversy at meetings held by the local authorities of Swansea Town and the surrounding districts it was openly alleged against me that I had used my influence as a member of the government to ensure that the Plant should be sited at Trostre in preference to Velindre.

"I was in a difficulty. I could not reply in public and I was counselled by both the Prime Minister and Stafford Cripps to remain silent. Meanwhile Stafford handled questions on the matter in the House. However, it was an unpleasant experience —all the more so as one of those who was bitter about it was fellow coal-miner and miners' M.P., D. R. Grenfell, the Member for Gower in which constituency Velindre was situated. In the end it came out alright. The Company reverted to their plan to build the two Cold Reduction Plants, one at Trostre and the other at Velindre. Both proved to be very successful enterprises.

"All this happened a long time ago (I write this in 1972) and all through the years I kept silent. When, after my retirement from the office of Secretary of State for Wales in 1966, I sat down to write my autobiography, I was tempted to include the story of Trostre and Velindre, but finally I decided to omit it from my published book, *Page from Memory*. However, in retrospect I feel proud to have been privileged to join my Welsh Parliamentary colleagues in securing that the first strip-mill in Britain was built at Ebbw Vale. The nearness of Ebbw Vale was a decisive factor in the subsequent decision to locate the second integrated plant at Llanwern in Monmouthshire. Now both the Margam and the Spencer (Llanwern) works are owned by the Nation and operated by the British Steel Corporation. I am also proud that I worked to ensure the 'Tinopolis' was not forgotten. Llanelli still has a secure place in the industry to which its workers and its citizens have given a century of service. We can still join together in singing 'Sospan Fach' . . .''

As a native of Llanelli (when Jim Griffiths was putting on record his account of the affair the bilingual changes had not come into effect and the townspeople still spelled it with a 'y') I knew to what he was referring. Llanelli-ites are justly proud of the song which has become known world-wide and which symbolised a closely-knit community. But the town's century-long affiliation to the steel and tinplate industries is no more. It has become a thing of the past and where once stood works and mills pulsating with energy, the heartbeat of a thriving community, there is hardly a building left to remind one of the vast and harrowing changes which have brought in their train a complete transformation of the town and its people. That secure basis in iron and steel to which Jim Griffiths referred did not obtain, regrettably.

I still cherish the memories of my early days among the steel and tinplate workers with their special camaraderie. But the harrowing memory of Dai Grenfell reduced to tears also remains vividly within me.

Jim Griffiths' contribution to the saga of Welsh strip-mills and the run-down of the old tinplate industry in West Wales, evokes many memories.

From the first day when I realised that, as a Lobby Correspondent, *I* could have some part to play in influencing government and public thought towards the rescue of a long-established and traditional tinplate industry in my birthplace, and neighbouring parts of South Wales, I seized every opportunity to press home the need.

I wrote countless pieces for my paper, and broadcast as many times over the air, to sustain public interest in the threats to jobs and the general sociological well-being in the tinplate areas. I supplied M.P.s with fodder for Parliamentary Questions and they responded willingly, albeit they recognised, too, the advantages of personal involvement in publicity for the cause. After all, publicity is the lifeblood of any M.P. or public figure. As Nye Bevan so aptly put it, "To be mentioned, whether good or bad, is better than never to be mentioned at all." In those early days there were many M.P.s, including Welshmen not representing Welsh constituencies, who felt very strongly about the threatened demise of the old hand-mills.

Among these, in particular, was Harold Davies, the then Labour M.P. for Leek in Staffordshire (Later Lord Davies), and a leading left-winger who had plenty of clout in the party and in the country. He had been urging the Attlee government to take a strong stand with General Chiang Kai Shek's China government to sustain the import of Welsh-produced tinplate for his country's canning industry. Welsh tinplate produced on hand rolling-mills had always been acknowledged as the best of its type, and China had been the best traditional customer. But the processes of canning had undergone a rapid and substantial change in the immediate post-war years, coupled with an inevitable increase in the production costs of Welsh tinplate. In any case, General Chiang had other, more momentous problems facing him than the canning industry in China. He was being menaced by the Communists led by Mao Tse Tung.

Neither the Labour nor the succeding Conservative governments were able to improve the trade, and the industry staggered on to total collapse, to be overtaken by more sophisticated and far more costly mills whose targets were the car and its ancillary industries.

As much as anything else I had been fired to press the cause of the ailing industry by memories of my early youth in Llanelli, whose proud motto, "Ymlaen Llanelly", was symbolic of the great post First World War growth in the production of tinplate on which the town's prosperity was founded and its title, "Tinopolis", rightly based.

In those halcyon days of the industry Llanelli was to tinplate what Dawson City was to gold. Indeed, many of its older inhabitants can probably still remember that one of the between-the-wars steel-works established in the town was nick-named "Y Clondiec" (The Klondyke) because of the very high wages earned there. Regrettably, that went the way of the other heavy industry works in the town and its outlying districts.

My earliest recollection of the old handmills and the thriving steel and tinplate industry of the town was the illuminating, red-streaked, sky above the town at evening time. When the furnaces of the huge steel-works at Morewoods and the Bury and others were being tapped, and the molten metal channelled into receptacles, their glow was trapped above and reflected onto the town like some magnificent aurora borealis. Fingers of red leapt across the sky, sometimes so vividly that even on the darkest night it was possible to read the newspaper headlines. They cast a great beauty around and it served as a constant reminder that this was the lifeblood of a growing community of some 40,000, and the source of their prosperity.

As those shafts of vermilion gradually lessened and phased out, ultimately to disappear altogether, so their absence acted as a reminder to the "Sospanites", as they have long been known, that the good times were coming to an end. No longer would it be possible for the young lads to experience and enjoy, as I and my contemporaries had sixty years previously, the fascination of watching the old tinplaters fashioning their products by hand and heavy graft. One of our simple enjoyments which never failed to fill me with awe around the age of ten to twelve years was watching the white-hot strips of reduced steel being cold-rolled into thin plate ready for tinning and conversion into tinplate.

The "handlers" as they were known (there were first and second hands) would deftly catch white-hot strips of metal in long iron tongs as they snaked across iron-plated floors from the furnaces and feed them into the reducing mills. It was hard and dangerous work, calling for a great deal of skill. The second hand would catch the strip as it emerged and fling it across to the "doublers", who would bend it over and feed it back into another stand of mills. And so it would go on, without stopping, through eight-hour shifts, night and day.

It was at night time that the show was seen at its best. My favourite spot was the Marshfield, and the Old Lodge works, which lay open to full public view from the main thoroughfare, Station Road, which linked the railway station with the town centre. I spent many hours admiring the skills and bravery of those men for whom one slip, (and such slips did happen), meant serious burns and injuries. In retrospect, and with a clearer image in the mind as I write about those days, I do not wonder that I took so much upon myself in the early days in the Lobby to publicise the plight of the industry. I only wish the outcome had been happier. But today there remains little or nothing to remind the inhabitants or visitors to the town of those great industrial and prosperous days. No edifices stand as memorials—the demands of development, in the name of "progress", have been too great. The days of the steel and tinplate booms are but memories for those who personally experienced them.

In later years there was another cause to which I sought to rally South and West Wales M.P.s—the need for an expansion in the steel industry to meet the prophesied demand arising from the rebuilding of a war-torn Europe and the development of the Third World. This became acceptable to the Conservative governments of Sir Anthony Eden and Harold MacMillan. It also fitted well into the pattern of the return of the vast steel industry from public to private ownership.

In Wales the giant Steel Company of Wales, under the chairmanship of Sir Julian Pode, submitted an ambitious scheme for a £1,000 million steel complex within the Principality. This was to be a major slice of the government's expansion plans for heavy industry, and sufficient indications had been forthcoming to confirm its benevolent acceptance by No. 10 Downing Street. Signs of a struggle over its location started emerging among M.P.'s from the various industrial areas north and south of the Wash, from Scotland and from Wales. This was to be the world-beater in modern, ultra-sophisticated and fully-integrated steel plants.

It was from this background that emerged the story now being revealed for the first time. Early in 1957, M.P.'s became excited over hints concerning a new multi-stand mill, even larger than the Margam giant with its added strip-mill facilities. It became known that S.C.O.W. was anxious to get things moving and was urging the need for a speedy decision. The Company had taken preliminary steps in the context of their plan by undertaking their own surveys of possible sites in Wales. Although their actions were closely guarded and highly confidential, occasional leaks whetted many appetites on the backbenches at Westminster.

I was entering the Members' Lobby one day when I was stopped by Rev. Llewellyn Williams, then M.P. for Abertillery and a Llanelli boy. We had attended the same school, Stebonheath, at about the same time and during his time at the House—regrettably he died suddenly in his middle years—we preserved a very close friendship and admitted our partisanship towards Llanelli. Llew was Pastor of King's Cross Welsh Chapel in London

and had the ear and confidence of many prominently placed ex-
patriates. He told me that he had heard, from an unimpeachable
authority, that the Steel Company of Wales ''at the highest
level'' was ready to advise the government that the new project
should be sited at Kidwelly, only ten miles from Llanelli and
the Trostre mills. This was great news, but I was sworn on
Lobby terms not to reveal the source of the information or who
was ''the highest level'' in the Company favouring this location. Sufficient, however, that a considerable amount of money
had been spent in boring and surveys and these had come up
with a final choice—the ''Flats'' at Kidwelly.

My exclusive on this story appeared in the *Western Mail* and
aroused considerable interest. At the same time as filing the
story, I put through a personal phone-call to Selwyn Samuel,
Town Clerk of Llanelli, another schoolboy contemporary of
both Llew and myself and another personal friend since we had
virtually shared desks in Bigyn Primary School. I suggested to
him that the Borough Council should be alerted to get in their
first claim. Kidwelly was sufficiently close to be regarded as
part of the Llanelli rural area—which it became a few years
afterwards under the reorganisation of local government. The
project could absorb all of the town's growing numbers of un-
employed, and more, and give a much-needed boost to the local
economy.

That was the beginning of long and bitter infighting over one
of the richest prizes in Britain's post-war industrial development. Selwyn Samuel and his officials, loyally aided by the
Borough's councillors, worked hard to sustain the initiative
they had secured by the early and inside information I was able
to feed back. But a tight rein was being kept on inside activities
at both government and Company level as they became aware
of increasing political influences at work at Westminster and in
the constituencies in Wales connected with the steel industry.

There were numerous deputations from the Llanelli Borough
Council to London, meetings with locally involved M.P.'s and

possible allies in the struggles ahead at Westminster, and contacts were made in Whitehall. Eveything that could be done to land the prize was done. Rarely did a meeting in London take place that I was not informed about either beforehand or immediately afterwards. The passages from the Central Lobby of the House of Commons to committee rooms and to the Strangers' Cafeteria on the Terrace level had been well trodden by Selwyn Samuel and me before or after these meetings when we met over a pot of tea to discuss progress.

It was about this time that I became aware of the strong feelings among the predominantly Labour M.P.s about the siting of the proposed works. In a very short time it was clearly defined as an East-versus-West issue, it being taken for granted that the project *would* end up in Wales. There was no doubt about the West Wales M.P.s supporting the Llanelli bid. Those to the east of the Vale of Glamorgan, however, were of the view that such a development should be located to the east of Margam, which was at that time the central point of Welsh steel and strip-mill production. Already the future of the Cardiff- and Newport-based steel works was causing some anxiety and no doubt the eastern sector M.P.s had to have regard for this.

At the same time my old friend, Dai Grenfell, for no clear-cut reason, flung another spanner into the works. There was no doubting, however, that his observations at this crucial time must have had an effect on the eventual outcome. He called attention to the vast reserves of best anthracite coal which, according to him, lay untapped beneath the "Flats". There would be no way, he claimed, that the National Coal Board would allow industrial development on the surface which would prevent future working of the coalfield. If what Dai Grenfell contended was right then, the "Flats" could be nothing more than a sterile area for development since at that time,—again according to the man whose knowledge of the Welsh coalfield and the working of coal was based on a long and practical association with the industry—it would be too difficult and costly to work the coal. This was due to the encroachment of the Bury Estuary tides and possible massive flooding. Although it was suggested later that Dai had acted in this way because the loss of the proposed Velindre works to Llanelli still rankled, I do not think this was so. He never admitted it to me, although we discussed the issue several times, but some damage had been done and alternative proposals to Kidwelly undoubtedly made a stronger appeal.

It was to this background that the controversy and the tug-of-war between East and West Wales M.P.s developed. Gradually the prospect of the project going to Kidwelly weakened. Clearly marked lines were drawn between those to the east and west of Port Talbot and alternative sites east of Cardiff were offered. These included the eventual choice, Llanwern, where the Spencer Works was eventually built, but in the run-up to the final decision the contesting M.P.s fought over it like dogs over

Inspecting the Site of Llanwern.

a bone. A consensus among Welsh M.P.s, which could well have ensured that the whole complex came to the Principality —east or west—became impossible and in the process the S.C.O.W. original proposal for a single complex was changed by the government.

The door was opened to Prime Minister Harold Macmillan to do something for his native Scotland, and at the same to solve a difficult problem which had beset the government.The Scottish steel industry needed a shot in the arm. The Welsh wrangle could provide it. He got his Cabinet to approve a scheme to hive off part of the project and to set it up in Ravenscraig. It was an astute move which hit the warring Welsh M.P.s very hard, but there was nothing that could be done to restore the project as a whole to Welsh soil. The Wentloog Marshes between Cardiff and Newport, which had figured as the likely alternative to Kidwelly, gave way to Llanwern, and Scotland got its unexpected bonus. That's how it happened.

Chapter 15: Some Famous Stories and Characters

Faux Pas

Looking back forty years to when the Press Gallery was being reformed after the extremely difficult six years of war and the rebuilding of the blitzed House of Commons, the difference in the methods and facilities of this highly specialised work has been astonishing. I do not think that any of my older colleagues in the Gallery would dispute that for those engaged in reporting Parliament today, things are considerably easier. I won't say simplified or less exacting, but at least it is less of a probability today that reporters will turn in reports which are misleading or incorrect owing to mishearing, or failing to hear at all, what is being said on the Floor of either House.

The installation of microphones has virtually cured that ailment of long-suffering Gallery members who used to crane their heads to catch what was being said above the hubbub of roused and raised voices. One had to adapt oneself to this condition and acquire and perfect a "parliamentary ear". The House of Lords had a shocking reputation for bad acoustics, and it has to be remembered that, for the first six years after the war, and before the new House of Commons Chamber was completed, M.P.s met in their Lordship's abode. The Press Gallery in the Chamber had been temporarily installed in the front few seats of the Public Gallery, from which the view of the Floor was partly obstructed by some brass or gilded rails originally provided to protect their Lordships from being pelted from a great height by irate onlookers. Such things *had* happened in the old days, but the nearest one gets to it nowadays is the dissemination of leaflets by the few demonstrators or campaigners who manage to elude the watchful eyes of officials.

Without the benefit of microphones and hearing-aids reporters suffered terribly, especially when M.P.s became embroiled in across-the-floor ructions. The Lobby Correspondents were less unfortunate only in that it was not their responsibility to report debates, only to interpret the ebb and flow and to sum up what the respective Front Benches had contributed. I always felt particularly sorry for the reporters, more so than for Hansard, who were in a more favoured position in the front row of the Press Gallery and who, in any case, could depend on their accounts being checked and corrected—not altered, though—by the speakers if necessary.

The bad acoustics resulted, from time to time, in unavoidable errors and Hansard, whose job it is to record every word spoken from the Floor of the House, was by no means immune from these. For instance there is the classic from one of Winston Churchill's more flowery orations. Readers of Hansard were surprised to elicit the following Churchillian advice: "Let's not embrace the huntsman while he is stewing the rabbits". The actual peroration was, "Let's not embrace the *helmsman* whilst he is *shooting the rapids*".

It is not known who was responsible for another oft-quoted misreport from the House of Lords, where one Noble Lord was recorded as stating, "They are as thick as thieves in Balham Broadway" when what he actually said, a quotation from Milton's *Paradise Lost*, was "Thick as autumnal leaves in Vallombrosa". Mixed metaphors abound in the Hansard volumes: "Mr. Speaker," said an Irish Member during the more robust days of Parnell, "I smell a rat. I see it floating in the air. Let us nip it in the bud." And what of the brave Scottish M.P. who reminded the House of Commons that, "Many a brave heart beats beneath the kilt of a Cameron Highlander"! From the annals of the House of Lords comes a saying related to a defence debate when the then Lord Cork and Orrery, breathing pure salt air and pressing home his point, declared, "We are a nation of sea-dogs. Let us see to it that our sea-legs are never cut from beneath our feet." There is no doubt that, if one had the time and the facility to browse through the parliamentary records from both Houses, one would find a veritable feast of mixed metaphors.

J. H. Thomas

Nothing excited me more in my early days at Westminster than to listen to and record the nostalgic memories of long-serving M.P.s and Members of the Upper House. I sought their company avidly on the Terrace during the warm summer evenings. Access to the Terrace was one of the most coveted of the Lobby Correspondent's privileges and there was no place more rewarding than this sanctuary to which Members adjourned after a tiring day . . . or to get away from public gaze. I would find them there, relaxed and vying one with the other in accounts of their personal involvement in events which were, or would be, of great historical significance. These were the tail-enders of a Parliamentary era before the advent of the "professional politician", a development which changed everything! Stories of some of the great characters, going back to First World War days, were always a delight. Then there were those who were about to retire, and those who had just retired but were still much in the public eye.

Jimmy (J. H.) Thomas, a member of one of Ramsay MacDonald's Cabinets, was one character about whom many stories were told. He was the one involved in the scandal of a Budget leak when he was Chancellor of the Exchequer. He had held several high offices of State, and was also one of the real Court favourites of King George V and Queen Mary. Down to earth, like the engine driver he had been before he entered Parliament as Labour Member for Newport, Jimmy Thomas' situations were the subject of many tales on the Terrace. His son, Leslie, the Conservative M.P. for Canterbury, became a very good friend of mine in the 'fifties and took pride that his father's reminiscences were so often revived in Terrace tête-a-têtes.

Jimmy, it was said, became a great friend of King George and Queen Mary and was a frequent guest at Buckingham Palace. It was during his term as Chancellor of the Exchequer, and when the economy in the mid-twenties was at a very low ebb, that he was asked by the King how he saw the future. Bluntly, as always, Jimmy replied, ''If I were you, Sir, I'd put the Colonies in the Queen's name, it's as bad as that.''

He purveyed many stories relating to his visits to the Palace and would declare that, on one occasion, he found Queen Mary particularly sympathetic when he was explaining some of his more difficult Budget problems. The Queen, also, was well known for her outspoken epithets and was in the habit of calling a spade a spade. According to Jimmy she replied, ''Yes, Mr. Thomas, it fair breaks your bloody heart, don't it.'' Jimmy's retort: ''Thanks, Ma'm, that cheers me up a lot.''

The one I like best, as more in keeping with what was said about him, was of Jimmy at the Lord Mayor of London's banquet. Warm-hearted and always gushing with help and advice, he apparently felt some sympathy towards an Oriental gentleman seated next to him at the top table, where he was a guest as Secretary of State for the Colonies. In his best ''Chinese'', Jimmy, asked politely, ''Likee soupee?'' and was satisfied with the confirmatory nod. Later, he confessed, he was surprised when the Oriental gentleman stood up to reply to the Toast to the Guests. This he did in faultless Oxford English, then, turning to Jimmy with a polite acknowledgement, he enquired, ''Likee speechee?'' And so the Terrace ranconteurs went on . . . and on . . . and on.

Cut-and-Thrust

The ordeal of an M.P.'s Maiden Speech, his or her first participation in the debates of the House on catching the Speaker's eye, and the avoidance of unparliamentary language, were frequently subjects of discussion. It was there I heard for the first time, in connection with the latter, the Churchill euphemism for a lie. ''Liar'', applied to any Honourable Member on the Floor of the House, is unparliamentary. Churchill got around that problem by referring to a ''terminological inexactitude''.

No one, I gather, was more adept at surmounting this type of difficulty than Disraeli who, according to the records, when called to order by Mr. Speaker for stating that half the Cabinet were asses responded, in his customary languid manner, "I withdraw, Sir. Half the Cabinet are NOT asses."

As for the Maiden Speech ordeal, there is an added difficulty caused by the accepted rule of the House that it should not be of a controversial character. It takes some M.P.s years to pluck up the courage to speak. Others eventually have to respond to constituency enquiries of "When?", because every Management Committee in the country likes to see its M.P. "quoted in the House". In my time I have known an M.P. to take five years before making the plunge, and some have succumbed to the ordeal and become virtually tongue-tied. The most notable parallel, I would say, was Mr. Gladstone. I have seen the record of his maiden speech when, apparently, the G.O.M. suffered an acute attack of nerves. The Official Report says of him only that "he made a few remarks which were not audible in the Gallery". Today it would have to be a most inept or inexperienced reporter who would turn in such a comment!

The main problem nowadays is that the Gallery is more likely to pick up remarks which it is not intended should be heard, so sensitive are the microphones on the Floor of the House. Many an aside intended only for private consumption on the benches has been picked up and could have meant an embarrassing situation for someone; but I have never known a case where one has been deliberately published in the day's reporting. Ministerial stumers, however, are fair game and they occur surprisingly more often than a casual attendant at the House might imagine. A favourite of mine is the gaffe committed by Stanley Evans, then Labour M.P. for Wednesbury, during one of his early appearances as Parliamentary Secretary at the Ministry of Agriculture, Food and Fisheries. Stanley was a bluff, hearty individual. "Self-made and proud of it," he used to say, and he was in fact a popular Member. If anything he may have been a little too indulgent within his department. He became known as "Featherbed Evans" because, during a tussle with the farmers, he quite uncharacteristically accused them of having been "feather-bedded" by his own party and his own Minister, Tom Williams (who, incidentally, was distinguished as the Minister who always wore a bow-tie). Another Labour M.P., George Dagger of Abertillery, also invariably favoured a bow-tie, but *he* never aspired to front-bench status).

Stanley's faux pas, which he carried to the end of his days and for which he was the butt of his colleagues during the remainder of his time in the House, was committed when he rose to answer a parliamentary question. A lady M.P. had called attention to the unhygienic condition of an abattoir in her Midlands constituency . . . I believe it was in the Wolverhampton area. Intent on making a good impression at the Dispatch Box, and with the deference he always tried to show to his questioners, unless they became objectionable, Stanley gallantly offered his personal attention to the complaint. "If the honourable lady will give me the address of this particular slaughter-house, I will go into it at once," he declared. The House immediately dissolved into laughter and delighted Tories kept up a barrage of advice. "The sooner the better," they hooted, "and take the government with you!"

Among the first advice I got from well-meaning colleagues was to be on the alert against seizing on the double-entendres which one hears from time to time in the House, some by accident, others by design. As an example I was given the story of the irate woman Member who complained to the Speaker after an abortive exchange during Question Time. In sheer frustration, and appealing for the protection of the Chair, she declared, "Every time I come in contact with the Rt. Honourable gentleman (the Minister) I find myself up against a brick wall." The House simply exploded and the embarrassed lady quickly resumed her seat. To mention an incident like this in a report from parliament was viewed with great displeasure by the majority of backbenchers who, rightly I believe, regarded such reference as bringing the House into disrepute. It wasn't worth the hassle to file such a story.

Although the Press Gallery always takes the greatest care in factually and correctly reporting the business of the House, especially Question Time, which always takes place before the House moves into its debates, there are times when a little licence is taken. This is particularly so when Ministers trip up at the Despatch Box. Although the Minister must bear full responsibility for his replies and statements to the House, it is no secret that their preparation is the responsibility of his private office. A good and dutiful Secretariat is worth its weight in gold to a Minister for the protection and support it provides in his briefs. The value of these briefs is usually measured by the skill of Civil Servants in anticipating what supplementary questions will be forthcoming to the Minister's reply. By common practice an experienced M.P. reserves the real sting in the tail of a seemingly harmless question on the Order Paper for the supplementary. A good Parliamentary Secretary can assist his Minister by anticipating what this could be and preparing him for it. Sometimes, however, things go wrong.

There was, for example, the case of the too-helpful Civil Servant who wrote into the Ministerial reply a few words of caution. ''Say as little as you can as (the questioner) is a damn nuisance,'' he had pencilled in. In the heat of the exchanges, and under considerable baiting from the other side, the unfortunate Minister was mortified to realise that the first part of the advice was being included in his reply. He made a recovery, but the House realised what had happened and the Opposition greatly enjoyed the poor chap's discomfort.

For a newcomer to the Front Bench, batting for the government from the Despatch Box can be an awesome experience. The time-honoured sport of baiting the Minister is a long-established part of the parliamentary scene and although generally the House of Commons is generous and understanding where errors or shortcomings are forced upon such an individual, it shows the characteristics of a savage animal at bay when it feels it is being deliberately misled. Also open to a savage mauling is any lacklustre or weak performance by a Minister or his Shadow. Again, much can depend on the Civil Servants' advices. There was the instance where a too-helpful P.S. tendered, at the tail of the reply to the anticipated supplementary, "This reply is not so hot, but I think it will get by . . ." In his flustered state the Junior Minister blurted out the first part and the House collapsed with laughter because Members on both sides realised how it had happened and were sympathetic. There are times, too, when an inexperienced Junior can find himself out of his depth and even the most perspicacious advisers fail to anticipate correctly. There is a formula for this sort of occasion and when resorted to properly it is accepted by the House. A Minister in trouble may say, "I must have notice of that question." It means,—"I don't know the answer but I'll get it for you."

But again, this goes wrong sometimes. On one occasion Miss Ellen Wilkinson, having been given an answer which was anything but a monument of clarity, persisted in demanding, "What does that mean?". The fumbling victim, a figure of abject misery, finally succumbed. "I must have notice of that question," he pleaded. This is an example which has been handed to young Ministers as the type of situation which the House will not tolerate with sympathy.

Most gaffes of this kind happen during Question Time, the first hour of the daily sitting of the House of Commons. The Houses of Parliament have been described as "the best and most exclusive Club in the world", but there is even more truth in the saying that Question Time is the best value in entertainment in London. The daily packed audience bears testimony to this. Some regard it as a safety-valve enabling M.P.'s on all sides to let off steam. Often it would appear to be so, judging from the raucous and utterly unparliamentary attitudes and behaviour on the backbenches. Since the House of Commons proceedings have been broadcast from time to time, public opinion has been sharply focussed on M.P.s apparently rowdy behaviour. It isn't really quite like that. The function of Question Time is basic to the whole fabric of our democracy. It is the key which frequently opens the door, in full public gaze, to issues, problems and situations, controversial and otherwise, as they affect the nation. Questions on all kinds of situations are permissible provided they come within the responsibility of a Minister of the Crown. Even the Prime Minister is not above backbench probing. In fact this invariably is the highlight of the occasion, though for only fifteen minutes in the hour twice a week during the sessional sittings. In this way both sides seek to test the strength and efficiency of the government in power. It would be a sad, indeed irresponsible act if this feature of our parliamentary activities was removed, or even reduced to a once-a-week session as is suggested from time to time.

An Irate Emperor

One day, during my early years at Westminster, I was told a memorable story by a Lobby colleague whom I and others held in the highest regard.

The House had been very tiresome and most M.P.s seemed to have gone away. Freddy Truelove, Political Correspondent of the *Daily Despatch*, and I were alone in the Members' Lobby just waiting for the rising of the House. I put in a very natural grumble about having to wait about in case something happened, which in my view seemed most unlikely. Freddy, a good deal older than I and, with a fatherly concern, I suppose, replied that the most unlikely things tended to happen when least expected. ''For instance . . .'' he began. I could see he wanted to talk, so I became a very patient listener. Well, there wasn't anything else I could do!

As he went on, however, I became more interested in what he was saying, and before I left Westminister that night, well after midnight, I had scribbled down the story he had to tell. Which is why I can relate it now.

It was around 1926, and he was walking down Whitehall to the House of Commons. Just past Downing Street he caught up with the then Labour Home Secretary, Joe Clynes, also making his way to Westminster from a Cabinet meeting. They knew each other very well through their Lobby relationships. The Home Secretary was in a hurry and, according to Freddy, complained that his annual duty trip to the Channel Islands had been upset because of some contentious Cabinet Committee chaired by Prime Minister Ramsay MacDonald.

Apparently the future of India had been discussed, with strong pressure for legislation in the next session granting Home Rule. It may have been that Joe Clynes, preoccupied with the upset of his Channel Islands visit, had not considered the importance of his comment or perhaps assumed that Lobby Correspondents were aware of the subject coming up before Cabinet. After all, there were fewer correspondents then and the relationships were much closer.

The *Daily Despatch* carried Freddy's story and gave it front-page headline treatment. The repercussions were swift, surprising, and severe. There was a peremptory summons from Buckingham Palace to Downing Street. Prime Minister MacDonald was required immediately for audience with the King. Their meeting was brief and, according to a report from the Cabinet Office, not lacking in outspoken comment as an irate King George V demanded an explanation why he, the Emperor of India, had not been informed of his government's aspirations for that country. It verged on a constitutional crisis and left Ramsay MacDonald "visibly shaken".

In turn, a furious Prime Minister summoned his aides on his return from the Palace, and demanded to know who had leaked the story. "I was just getting ready to leave for work when a couple of Special Branch men arrived,'' Freddy went on. ''They wanted to know where my story had come from. I was scared, of course, but I refused to give the source of the information.''

He had become really frightened when he was told cryptically that he would have to tell because the demand came from ''the very top'', whoever that might be. He was taken to Scotland Yard insisting that the information had been given to him on Lobby terms and he was unable to break that confidence. However, he agreed to do so if he could be released from the confidence, which meant a phone-call in private. This was allowed and the Home Secretary's private secretary was contacted. He was asked to get in touch with Mr. Clynes immediately, but said he could not because the Home Secretary was on one of the Channel Islands.

The urgency of the situation having been explained to the Home Office, Freddy was allowed to make contact personally. Joe Clynes, who was on Alderney, admitted the indiscretion immediately and later made his full explanation to the Prime Minister and his Cabinet colleagues. There was no question of resignation but in view of the Sovereign's anger discussion on the future of India was dropped.

Twenty years later I was in the House of Commons, as was Freddy, listening to Clement Attlee explaining Labour's fulfilment of its commitment to Home Rule for India, and wondering whether the breakup of the British Empire would have been more greatly accelerated, and the result of the Second World War been different, had Freddy Truelove not met Joe Clynes that fateful day, and had the *Daily Despatch* not carried the banner headlines of a story which came from a casual exchange between a Minister and a Lobby Correspondent.

Cosy Exchanges

A good and trusting relationship between Ministers, M.P.'s and a Lobby Correspondent together with the newspaper's executives, has always been regarded as essential to a mutually satisfactory basis of operation and co-operation. It was with this in mind that I and my then Editor, David Cole, decided on a series of *Western Mail* and *Echo* dinners at the House of Commons, at least one to be held each session.

There was a ready response from M.P.s on both sides of the House. In order, however, to achieve the best results, David and I agreed that, so far as the newspapers were concerned, it would be better if we played host to a balanced table; that is, get together as near as possible a representation of the make-up of the Floor of the House. Our problem then was that, since the functions were to be exclusive to *Welsh* M.P.s, we had to bear in mind that Labour M.P.'s were in the ratio of three-to-one to Conservative and Liberal Members. This could mean that the Tory and Liberal M.P.'s might be invited for a second time before the Labour tail-enders had sampled any of our hospitality. It wasn't long before we were holding the dinners more than once a session, with the two editors and the Managing Editor jointly hosting them.

Without question these dinners became an important part of the Welsh parliamentary scene. They were a success from the outset as an exercise in public relations. The across-the-table contacts and free flow of ideas and conversation broke new ground and before long the word went around. After a couple of years some of the other regional newspapers with Lobby Correspondents followed suit and within five years at least half a dozen of these sessional functions were being booked with the House of Commons Catering Department.

It was the intention from the beginning that the around-the-table conversations would enable the editors and Managing Editor to engage in a completely uninhibited exchange of views in the cosy atmosphere of one of the smaller dining rooms off the Terrace. With a mixture of M.P.'s from all parties present, it would be unlikely that any one party would be allowed to get across unchallenged any claims for its particular policies or its independent projections concerning constituencies.

A Cosy Dinner at the House, 1968.

After the first couple of functions the dinners settled down as an established event in the sessional calendar. They were enjoyable as well as mutually informative and this was because they were conducted along Lobby lines. Nothing was ever printed and there were never, to my knowledge, any inquests among M.P.s who attended on the subjects of our conversations. Indeed, they set such store by them that I was frequently reminded by M.P.s on both sides that they had not yet attended a dinner, or that it had been some time since the last invitation.

Many confidences were traded but never was one betrayed. The M.P.s were free, and they took every opportunity to exercise the freedom, to question the executives on their papers' policies, and often to hit hard against alleged bias in parliamentary and political coverage. One of the hardest-hitting exponents was Michael Foot, who made it clear that accepting the invitation in no way prevented him from lashing out at the

Western Mail, which he regarded still as the handmaiden of the coal-owners and an anti-socialist newspaper. This seemed strange to me, coming, as it did, from a former newspaper editor. The "coal-owners' paper" image still persisted among Labour M.P.s and, even today, there are some, who could not have known or had any personal connection with those times, who regard it with an inborn distrust. Nothing could be further from the truth and fortunately they are getting fewer with successive parliaments.

The dinners promoted an understanding between those who published and those who made political news and I cannot recall any instance of discord around the table, even when Geoff Rich, the *Echo* editor, was in his most provocative moods with the Tories. Eventually, however, they had to cease. Mounting costs of entertaining at the House of Commons forced me to call it a day. The intimate "C" and "D" dining rooms, which had so often rung with vibrant, but never hostile, exchanges among fifteen to eighteen diners amicably indulging in the art of conversation (which regrettably is practised too infrequently these days) surrendered their hospitality to the prohibitive charges.

However, the functions did not really end there. For a couple of years we continued outside Westminster. The venue was transferred to my home, "Four Winds", on the outskirts of Uxbridge and although the atmosphere lacked that Palace of Westminster something, the functions continued successfully. If only that spacious dining room in "Four Winds" could talk! Myfanwy, my wife, was an exemplary hostess, well known to all the guests. They were made to feel at home and our table for eighteen invariably resounded to the chatter of cross-party politics. The more serious talking followed and it is no false claim that more political confidences and ideas, mainly for the Principality, were exchanged at "Four Winds" than at any gathering outside the Cabinet Room at No. 10 Downing Street.

The last of a long line of editors to preside over these functions were Duncan Gardiner of the *Western Mail* and Geoff Rich, O.B.E., of the *Echo*, along with Managing Editor, David Thomas. Happy days! Without doubt those editors at that time must have been the best-informed politically in the whole country, yet, true to the ideals on which the dinners were launched, no one broke a confidence in print or otherwise, nor did anybody take unfair advantage. But they were privy to much of the reasoning which lay behind important political events and decisions.

The Guinea Club

An established function which always attracted the keenest competition among M.P.'s for invitations was the Guinea Club. This was a dining-club set up by a small group of Gallery and Lobby Correspondents, which met every third Tuesday of the month in Dining Room "A" on the Terrace level whilst the House was sitting. This venue was appropriate because it had been known in the Irish Days as "Parnell's Room", being the one where Irish M.P.'s met in the volatile days before Independence.

The idea was first mooted by Peter Midforth in 1956. He was then Parliamentary Correspondent of the *Birmingham Post*, and its London Editor. Peter's idea was to set up a dining-club similar to those enjoyed mainly by the Tory Party. Unlike those, which met outside Westminster, the Guinea Club would have regular in-session meetings to which politicians of all sides would be invited.

I was a founder-member of the Club, whose guiding rules then were that only one correspondent of any newspaper, either Lobby or Gallery, could be a member, and that the meetings would be, as it were, in camera. The title "Guinea Club" was chosen as representative of the number 21. So there were to be twenty-one members, it would meet on the twenty-first of the month (or the Tuesday nearest to that date) and the lunch would cost a guinea a head for a member and his one (maximum) guest.

The lunch would have a leading politician as chief guest and he would be encouraged to be outspoken and forthcoming on matters of current political controversy. One rigid rule was set and observed: what was said or revealed by the speaker was to be contained within the walls of Dining Room "A". Nothing was to be reported and nothing was to be said outside which would give any indication of whatever had been disclosed at the lunch. That rule has been maintained and strictly observed throughout the thirty years of the Club's existence. It was based on Lobby ethics and as such encouraged guest-speakers to open their minds and mouths to such an extent that perhaps no other body has ever been the recipient of so many confidences and exposures—from backbenchers right up to Prime Ministers.

I well recall the first lunch. Charles (later Sir Charles) Harris was the chief guest. At that time he was in charge of the Government Whips' Office at Downing Street and was a favourite with all Lobby Correspondents. He had been invited to talk about the secrets of his office and in order to give this trial-run its best chances of success we had all been asked to invite only Front Bench guests from both sides of the House. It was a power-packed occasion. My guest was Lord Mancroft, an Under Secretary at the Home Office who would later be a Guinea Club chief guest himself, with a striking reputation as a post-prandial speaker.

Charles gave a most impressive speech and not a word of it appeared in any newspaper, which encouraged us to put out further invitations. Next of what was to be, over the years, an illustrious list of speakers was Herbert Morrison. He proved more daring . . . but still not a word in the papers! This was an encouragement to Government and Opposition prominents whom Peter selected as carefully as a duellist choosing his weapons.

In 1957 it was my turn to be in the chair when Lord Attlee was the chief guest. He was the first of the Prime Minister guests. Except for Churchill and Sir Anthony Eden every Prime Minister has been the Club's guest. This was the only occasion when I found Clem Attlee to be more than mono-syllabic. My recollection is that he was quite cheerful and thought the Club a splendid institution based on the excellent motives of bringing pressmen and politicians together to rid them of their mutual distrust. In his time, of course, there had been the Sidney Stanley and Belcher scandals, and a number of leaks which had turned M.P.s against the Press. He made a witty speech but steered clear of the issues which had created the political dissensions in his days at No. 10. It was not in his character to dwell on those aspects of his governments, which was a disappointment. But his speech was the curtain-raiser to many from high places which produced highly confidential material.

One from outside the political field was Lord Goddard, who was Lord Chief Justice when he accepted the Club's invitation towards the end of 1959, and again I was privileged to be in the chair. Most of us assumed we were going to hear an erudite and deep-thinking speech on the legal system and the reforms then in hand, perhaps some criticisms of the government's handling of law and order. His Lordship, however, soon dispelled any thoughts of a pontifical address. During the lunch he launched into a succession of jokes and parodies of the Bar which would have done justice to a typical night out in a downtown hostelry. He possessed an astonishing fund of risqué stories which seemed quite out of place for a Chief Justice. But he was a jolly fellow and somehow managed to steer just wide of the most objectionable, and it *was* an all-male gathering!

His voice was so penetrating that long before he was called by me to address us, the entire table had become privy to his stories. Like expectant vultures soaring over a corpse, their appetites whetted by what they had already heard, they prepared for a feast.

The Club was treated to such a wealth of anecdotal accounts regarding the Courts, High and low, as I and others had never heard and, in my case, I suppose, will never hear again. The Viscount Boyd, formerly the Rt. Hon. Alan Lennox Boyd, Colonial Secretary, was at that lunch and expressed the wish to make his contribution as a chief guest of the Club. He was personally known to us all and Peter Midforth arranged it six lunches later.

That was the beginning of a long and interesting association between us. A member of the Guinness family, he had told them about this wonderful Guinea Club which was commanding a lot of attention at Westminster and the outcome was an invitation to the Club members to visit Dublin and tour the brewery as guests of the family. They did us proud from the moment we all got into a private aircraft at Heathrow until two days later when we were flown back. We must have made a good impression on our hosts, because we were ferried over again twice in the following three years, and also became guests of the family in London, at Park Royal. His tragic death in a motor accident some years later caused much grief to many of us. Viscount Boyd was in the habit of riding into New Palace Yard on fine summer days on the rolled-back tonneau of his chauffeur-driven car, waving to everybody just as if he was on an election campaign.

Another memorable function was the lunch at which Leslie Hale, the chubby Labour M.P. with the reputation for being the fastest talker in the House, put in his fastest-ever time. He would have defied the world's champion shorthand writer to a verbatim take. He spoke at about three hundred words per minute, but, as a lawyer, he was one of the most interesting speakers in the House. However, he was, in a sense, his own worst enemy. When he got carried away with his subject he would speed up and it became impossible to take a full note. At the Guinea Club lunch, he excelled anything he had previously done, and by intention; so much so that he had everyone in tears of laughter and possibly with half a dozen different interpretations of what he had been saying.

The pity is that we were not allowed in those days to use pocket-recorders in the Gallery. In any case, however, the acoustics were so bad I doubt whether a recorder would have picked up backbench speeches in sufficient strength to make them intelligible. In those days Gallery men had to cultivate the "House of Commons ear".

The use of a pocket-recorder did once play a special part in the unique outcome of one Guinea Club lunch. It was in 1974 that Tony Benn, then Shadow Minister for Energy, and already a left-wing rebel and a thorn in Harold Wilson's side, was invited to be chief guest. On this particular occasion we were meeting for the first time outside the House. There had been a row over the increased charges for Dining Room "A"—already they had broken through the guinea barrier by a very long way—and we had decided to try an outside venue. We arranged for it to take place at St. Stephen's, opposite Big Ben.

Everything went well to begin with. There was no complaint about the lunch and when it was over, as was our custom the chairman, this time Bill Greig, Political Correspondent of the *Daily Mirror* and then senior Lobby man, introduced Tony Benn. It was routine. We all knew him and everything about him that was worth knowing. He was among friends and everyday acquaintances. A few minutes later he had lost many of them.

Tony rose to speak, having made an ill-concealed attempt to ignore the Loyal Toast, and took from his pocket something which he placed on the table in front of him. "Members of the Guinea Club and friends . . ." he began. Suddenly, the chairman sprang to his feet to interrupt. He felt it right, he said, to inform the Club that Mr. Benn had placed a tape-recorder on the table, obviously to record what he was about to say. Bill was sorry to do this, but he reminded the Club he had uttered the usual formula in introducing the chief guest, namely that this was an occasion about which nothing would be written or discussed outside the room and that, in the confidence that it was being treated as on Lobby terms, our speaker would be free, and possibly be further encouraged, to speak frankly on his chosen subject. It was an insult to the Club and its guests, he went on, that for fear of being "misreported" or "misconstrued", and ignoring the long-standing Lobby rule, Tony Benn had chosen to bring in a tape-recorder and then place it on the table to record his speech. He invited Tony to remove "the offending object" and to allow the Club to carry on in the manner of its eighteen years' existence without any complaints.

Tony refused. He insisted that, as a figure in so many controversial issues, and a target for right-wing critics (whom he regarded as being in the majority in the Club) it was necessary he should have a full record of his remarks. He also pointed out that he had used the recorder for some time at all his public and other meetings and saw no reason to depart from his now-established system. Outcome of his refusal was that the chairman declared he was vacating the chair and invited those who shared his view to leave also. It was very embarrassing. Out of politeness to other guests—and also to Tony Benn, let it be said—some of us stayed on. But the lunch was a fiasco, the only time in its now near thirty years of existence that the Guinea Club failed to fulfil its function.

The Green Baize and Nye

One particular question keeps cropping up in my mind, and I cannot find a completely satisfactory answer to it! Were the ten or fifteen minutes we spent on the green baize the final turning-point in Nye Bevan's tempestuous career? Had he reached a different decision that day, could he have achieved his long-cherished ambition to become leader of the Labour Party by taking over from a deposed Hugh Gaitskell?

At the Crossroads: 'Nye' Bevan and Hugh Gaitskell.

What I do know is that I was with him, and we were alone, for that very short period of time in 1957 when he reached the crossroads (the final one of the many in his turbulent political life) on the highly controversial question of the H-bomb and the inflamed issue of the party's Ban-the-Bomb movement.

The issue which had been burning up his conscience and principles was whether, as deputy leader at that time of the Labour party, he should support the Gaitskell line of retaining the ultimate weapon as a deterrent. Or should he, instead, lead the unilateralist leftist move to scrap it, notwithstanding any agreements with or obligations to Britain's allies.

The occasion was that special Party Conference in Brighton when the whole world's attention was focussed on the Nye Bevan decision. He was then Shadow Foreign Secretary.

Michael Foot, author of the Bevan biography and the man who sought to drape the Bevan mantle around his shoulders when, three years later, he stood as candidate for Tredegar after the untimely death of Nye on the 6th July 1960, relates how Bevan confessed afterwards that on that afternoon on the Brighton platform he had faced the most tremulous, heart-broken audience of his life. He quotes him as saying, ''I knew this morning I was going to make a speech that would offend and even hurt many of my friends.'' But there is something about which Nye's biographer and his friends know nothing. Something which happened between that morning and mid-afternoon, when he faced his split audience, something which might well have had the final bearing on his decision because, as he admitted to friends afterwards, whichever side he had come down in favour of he would have been bound to evoke hostilities.

I can now reveal, for the first time, that I was with him during his last moments of terrible anguish and when he reached his decision. That decision was finalised, if not actually taken, as we aimlessly knocked around some snooker balls over the green baize.

I was in the headquarters hotel, which was strangely empty just after lunch, the delegates and the party leaders having gone back to the conference hall. I heard the click of snooker balls. Looking into the Billiard Room, I saw Nye, all alone, aimlessly flicking balls around the table. He looked up, saw me, saw that I was alone, and, perhaps out of embarrassment as much as anything, asked, ''Do you play, Dai?'' I did in those days, and pretty well too, though I say so myself!

We lined up the triangle without more ado. He was unusually quiet. I wanted to ask him why he was there and not at the conference, but for the first few minutes I contained myself. Then, as casually as I could, I asked, ''What are you going to say this afternoon?''

There was no reply, and I could sense that he was greatly troubled. We ''played'' for not more than ten or fifteen minutes. Then, suddenly, he put down his cue. ''Thank you,'' he said briskly. ''I've made up my mind and if you want to know you had better get back soon." Typical of him, he wouldn't let on before he had made the announcement official. I realised, as he was walking out, that he had been struggling with his inner self, but he would say nothing more.

When he did declare, about an hour later, which side he was taking, and that it was to stand alongside Hugh Gaitskell, it was not so much for keeping the H-bomb but that Britain should not unilaterally opt out of her obligations to her allies. As Michael Foot has already revealed, Nye's objective was not so much to *favour* the bomb as to find the most effective way of, as he had put it, "getting the damn thing destroyed".

Would that have been his decision had he gone straight to the conference hall after lunch and been subjected to the intense lobbying of his friends of the Left? After all, it was with them that he had had the greater and more effective alliances during his rumbustious campaigns against the Party leadership on many issues from his very first days in the House of Commons.

I like to think, after all these years, that those few minutes we spent over the green baize helped Nye to resolve the struggle of conscience which must have been eating him up. Clearly he knew it would be a parting of the ways with a large section of Labour Party opinion, and even that he would be branded a traitor to the true Socialist cause. However, as so many times in his chequered and militant career, Nye acted in what he considered to be the best interests of the Labour Party and its future.

With hindsight, I believe his reason at that vital Brighton confrontation was amply justified. Had he gone in other directions, his party might easily have reverted to the situation of the early twenties, with Gaitskell, a latter-day Ramsay MacDonald, leading his ferociously divided Party—to nowhere.

Strangely enough, of all the Welsh M.P.s with whom I was constantly in contact, since that was my prime responsibility in the Lobby, the one with whom I had the most tenuous link was Nye Bevan. He in particular hated the *Western Mail* and all that it had stood for as "the coal owners' journal". On a personal level we got on well enough, but I could never convince him that my paper had changed greatly in its political outlook and presentation since the war.

He would be helpful when I sought his help on general party issues, but when in government, or in matters concerning Wales, he could be bluntly discourteous. As, for instance, the night I had been expressly asked by my Editor, David Prosser, to contact him and find his reaction to and personal judgement on, a Conservative Party amendment to the Employment Bill then before the House and which had an important bearing on the mining-industry.

It took me hours to track him down and we eventually met in the Library Corridor. He walked me down towards the Speaker's Office whilst I put the points my Editor wanted clarified. Suddenly he turned angrily to me and said, "It's all right with you, Dai, (he had always, to my annoyance, called me this), but not for that bloody coal owners' paper. Tell him to go to Hell!" He turned and flounced away, leaving me "out of bounds" and quite taken aback by his vehemence. At other times he could be quite friendly, but he never accepted, as other members of the Welsh Labour Group did, that there was any special link between us.

I firmly believe that, had he not been struck down so suddenly and tragically in July 1960, less than three years after he had become deputy Party leader to Hugh Gaitskell, Nye would have reached the top and would have led his party back into government. Admittedly he had publicly rejected any personal aspirations to the leadership in 1957, but his partnership with Gaitskell had moved onto such firm ground that the question of leadership could just as easily have been re-opened and he would have accepted being drafted. Political history, however, will record how, within a year of Nye's death, Hugh Gaitskell too died and Harold Wilson took over the leadership and became the second post-war Labour Prime Minister.

One of the most emotional experiences of my life occurred when I was invited by the B.B.C. to act as link-man in the World Service broadcast of Nye's funeral. I was in Bush House, Kingsway, with a specially prepared biography of his personal political life. In the background were strains of Welsh hymns as mourners in their hundreds gathered on the mountain-top above Tredegar to pay their last respects to the man of whom it was said, "There will never be another like him from these parts." Occasionally, above the muted singing, could be heard the soughing of the wind. It brought a lump to my throat; I was on the brink of tears. Only with help from the producer, Havard Gregory, did I pull through. Later I was told the whole world had heard the broadcast and that it had been described as the most moving experience over the air.

The Man of Secrets

In 1963, on a bitterly cold day in January, I received an invitation to go down to Sussex to see Lord Hankey, known as the "Man of Secrets". He had been Secretary to the Cabinet during Lloyd George's war-time Premiership and for some time afterwards. As it turned out, that interview was one of the highlights of my career. I found he was indeed a man of many secrets, but he was prepared to talk to me about them, warts and all. He was publishing his memoirs and since a great deal of the book involved the "Welsh Wizard" (his description) he felt he could add information about L. G. that was omitted from his two volumes based on what the authorities at that time considered were his "too frank and comprehensive diaries". "Frank and comprehensive" he certainly turned out to be!

It was snowing heavily as I drove up to the cottage on the Downs and was admitted by an aged Lady Hankey into "the sanctum". Lord Hankey was then well into his eighties and his "sanctum" turned out to be a small room, unheated except for a small smoky oil-stove, and packed with books and files to such an extent that there was barely enough room for the two chairs we shared, he in his old easy-chair and I on an odd dining-room chair which proved uncomfortable in the extreme. But I was not there to relax. I wanted to know what he could tell me, about L. G. the man, the politician and the Statesman, that was not already known.

After the initial greeting and a welcome cup of tea he suggested that he should talk at random and I would take whatever notes I liked. Afterwards I would let him know which parts interested me and my readers. This was agreeable and off he went. It was not, in fact, a rambling exercise: he was astonishingly clear and precise as to dates and places. There was only one snag. He kept dropping off for brief snoozes every ten minutes or so. The amazing thing, however, was that, on waking, he simply went on (with a little prompting from me) from where he had left off. Our talk lasted about three hours. It should have been not more than two, and I must have shown considerable patience, because I had to wait each time for him to de-nap himself, and the fumes from that oil-stove were giving me a thumping headache.

Throughout our chat Lord Hankey sat in his easy-chair and wore an overcoat and a thick scarf. I couldn't understand it. Less than a week later, however, he was admitted to a local hospital and died, aged 86. I was the last, if not the only, journalist to interview him before he severed all links.

That interview gave me yet another instance of the Welsh language playing an important, indeed historic role in top-flight politics and affairs of State. Lord Hankey's reminiscences about L. G.'s association with his own appointed Deputy Secretary to the Cabinet, Dr. Tom Jones, father of Eirene (now Baroness) White, were fascinating. Dr. Jones had been brought to Whitehall from South Wales, where he had held an official trade union position, and, according to Hankey, L. G. and he constantly spoke Welsh, to the great annoyance of Hankey and other high-ranking officials.

Lloyd George often disappeared across the Channel during the latter stages of the war for *affaires d'amour* and off-the-record visits. On these occasions he always maintained close touch with No. 10 Downing Street, where Dr. Jones would be at hand to receive fixed-time calls from L. G.'s villa at Fécamp in Normandy. He was kept well in touch with home affairs by his trusty friend, and managed many decisions at this long range when the nation presumed its Prime Minister was still in London. These contacts were conducted in Welsh, and it might never have come to light but for a heated exchange one night at a meeting which included Clemenceau, "The Tiger", head of the French government.

Hankey mused over this story with relish. "You see," he told me, "the French had been tapping L. G.'s line, and when the issue of trust and confidence was raised at that meeting Clemenceau charged L. G. with not showing trust to his hosts by speaking in a tongue which could not be understood." It was his first intimation that the French were keeping him under surveillance, but the trips to Fécamp continued, as did the telephone-calls in Welsh.

Von Rundstedt

Being in the right place at the right time as a journalist is, more often than not, a stroke of good luck. I must confess, therefore, that I have enjoyed my fair share of it. A striking example was my meeting with Field Marshal von Rundstedt, Germany's master-strategist and the chief adversary of the Allied Command during the Second Front invasion of Europe. He it was who tried to execute Hitler's last gamble to turn the war after the Allies had secured a firm footing in their relentless advance towards Germany.

Rundstedt's counter-attack through the Ardennes in December 1944/January 1945, designed to force a wedge between the allied forces, and also to cut the American supply lines from

Cherbourg and other French ports, became the Battle of the Bulge. The military aspect is not something I can dwell upon, except for a brief personal involvement. What *has* mattered to me, however, is my meeting with von Rundstedt not much more than a year later.

After six and a half years' wartime service with the R.A.F., I was on demobilisation leave in January 1946 at home in Bridgend. We lived not more than half a mile from Island Farm, the then high-ranking German officers' Prisoner-of-War Camp, the very one from which the solitary German P.O.W. escape was attempted during the latter stages of the war. Part of the in-mates' daily exercise was a walk through the lanes of the picturesque Merthyr Mawr, under a strong military armed guard because several of them were awaiting their transfer to the Nuremberg War Trials. I, too, along with my wife and baby son, enjoyed walking those lanes when the weather permitted, and it was during one of these walks that I encountered a group of officers who were quite affable and in good spirits. In their midst was a tall, distinguished-looking and aloof officer of very high rank. It was Marshal von Rundstedt.

During the next few weeks my walks became more frequent and I suppose I became a more familiar figure, not only to the guards but to the officers as well. I was in civilian clothes and therefore rank did not matter. I was allowed to exchange the usual pleasantries with the prisoners (no one knew that I was a journalist shortly to resume his pre-war career).

I was determined to speak to von Rundstedt because I wanted to make a significant come-back as the *Western Mail's* man in Bridgend and the Vale of Glamorgan, (my position before the war). The opportunity came when his Adjutant, who spoke English and had several times passed the time of day with me, agreed to put my request to the Marshall "off the record". But, being the strict disciplinarian he was, it was suggested to me that I should first seek the permission of the Commandant and the War Office. Nonetheless, we did chat during some of the walks, mainly through Major (I think it was Ernst, but I cannot now be sure), his friendly Adjutant. I told him that I had been despatched to the Ardennes from Brussels, mentioning Bastognc and St. Hubert.

After discussing the possibilities, my editor requested War Office permission to interview von Rundstedt, but this was rejected. However, I wrote several pieces after that about Island Farm and my casual meetings with German officers, and I honestly believed von Rundstedt had accepted me, because he showed less aloofness towards the end of the association. I was told when he was to be transported to Nuremberg for trial, and was asked to be on Bridgend railway station for a farewell. It was at his request, I believe, that I was allowed on the platform before the train departed, though I was not allowed to speak to him or any of the others; there was too much Top Brass about at the time. But I was the only journalist allowed on the platform and a staff-photographer took a pictorial record!

Little had I realised, nearly two years earlier, as I sat in a troop-train along with many thousands of others from all services drafted from Brussels into the Ardennes between Christmas and New Year's day 1945, that I was destined one day to be an acquaintance of, and on speaking terms with, the one who was responsible for the Battle of the Bulge. As I have said, a journalist needs the luck of being in the right place at the right time!

Chapter 16: Prime Ministers I have known

One of my proudest claims must be that I have served in the Lobby under no fewer than nine Prime Ministers and, with only one exception, can claim to have been on more than just a nodding-acquaintance. The odd-one-out would be Winston Churchill who, except for a few social occasions, deigned not to associate with either the Lobby as a body or any of its members individually. Come to that, he had a very few, beyond his Ministers, whom he regarded as persona grata to the Churchill entourage, and with whom he would even pass the time of day outside the Chamber. It may have been, as was more than once suggested by his opponents, that his rejection by the voters in the 1945 General Election increased his bitterness and made him a very solitary figure in and around the corridors of Westminster.

Clement Attlee

First of the nine was Clement Attlee, who led the Labour landslide of 1945. He was not, at sight, an impressive figure in the House of Commons, either in debates or during the twice-a-week ordeal of Prime Minister's Questions, but he *was* one of the shrewdest. From the Press Gallery his high-pitched voice was clearly audible, but he was one of the most difficult speakers to take down in shorthand. His delivery and manner were sharp, clipped and staccato, and he seldom indulged in prolonged arguments—not even with his chief adversary, Winston Churchill.

One habit which seemed particularly odd to the onlooker from the galleries was his doodling. Attlee was a particularly fine doodler and his output was greater when the House was involved in sharp controversy, or sitting late, as it often was in those days. It's always a puzzle to visitors to the House of Commons to see occupants of the respective Front Benches lounging in their places with feet up on the Clerk's Table. It is a traditional right of their office dating back to the time of Cromwell and his Ministers, who used to attend the House in the Ironsides uniform, complete with spurs which used to be rested on the table. The actual table in use during those days remains in the Crypt at Westminster and shows clearly the marks of the rowells.

It was a posture which Clem Attlee favoured and he would habitually be found, with feet up, seemingly detached from what was happening around him, doodling on House of Commons headed note-paper. At the end of a long sitting which had gone on into the following morning, it was not uncommon for these doodles to be strewn around the Front Bench and there was much competition among the women cleaners, as they went into the Chamber, to snatch up the Attlee creations. No doubt there are still some around as souvenirs in various households.

Detached from things around him he may have appeared to the onlookers in his doodling moments, but detached from the realities of the moment he certainly was not, for he was known to spring to his feet to intervene whenever he disagreed with what had been said. Another quality, recognised by those who were close to him, and those who from time to time came under the lash, was his discipline. He was a forthright disciplinarian who acted swiftly and uncompromisingly against those who did not match up to the high standards he set and demanded.

For the whole of his first period of government Attlee orchestrated the vast operation of transferring the major industries and public utilities from private to public ownership. The great moral issue of Nationalisation sustained the massive Labour machine in Parliament for five years while its overwhelmingly strong majority provided an unassailable buttress against Opposition efforts to stem the tide. The minorities on the left were able to prosecute their own private principles and brands of ultra-socialism in the knowledge that the government party could safely withstand all attempts to remove it. The situation, however, inevitably created strains within the Parliamentary Labour Party. Petty revolts eroded the 1945 solidarity. Halfway through there was an attempt at what Herbert Morrison, then House of Commons Leader, and other members of the government, described as a Palace Revolution to replace Attlee by Ernest Bevin. It failed because bluff and honest Ernie wanted nothing to do with it and made this quickly clear in the most outspoken way. But it was symptomatic of the internecine strife which, at that time, was starting to tear the Parliamentary Party apart.

There were a few expulsions in the aftermath and only the Attlee discipline prevented matters from worsening. The effects could be measured by the 1950 General Election, which almost swept Labour out of office. It came back with a flimsy half-dozen majority and in 1951 the great public ownership bubble burst when Attlee had to go to the country again and the Conservatives romped home. For the Parliamentary Labour Party the next few years saw much bitter in-fighting before the rot could be stopped by the emergence of Hugh Gaitskell and his new-found ally, Nye Bevan, (whose Bevanite Group had outlived its declared purpose of keeping the Labour Party a ''true'' socialist party).

During his leadership Attlee's tight control of both the National and the Parliamentary Party had kept it intact despite the problems of minor insurrections, the ''Bevanites'' and the Communist Nenni Telegram affair. Insofar as his personal contact with the Lobby was concerned, he was a virtual stranger. True, Ministerial contacts with the Lobby at that time were in any case very infrequent. Most correspondents preferred to trawl the Lords and Commons in the traditional manner on their own, or in small groups. Only on the very rare occasion did the Prime Minister choose to make a personal appearance. Lobby contact had been delegated to Herbert Morrison and it was Wily Herbert who first cultivated it as the

sounding-board for some of Labour's more controversial legislation. He sought to make us the guinea-pigs of public opinion
with regard to certain legislation in the government pipe-line.
Mention of a measure at a Lobby meeting invariably meant
someone would file an "I gather . . ." story about proposed
government legislation. Reactions to this would be carefully
monitored and if they were critical the idea could be stillborn.

The nearest I can recall to a defences-down meeting between
Clem Attlee and the Parliamentary Press was on the occasion of
the formal opening of the new Parliamentary Press Gallery
premises towards the end of his Premiership. It was worthy of
record, and a framed photograph of the occasion, which also
includes Winston Churchill and Clement Davies, the Liberal
leader, hangs in the premises.

Churchill: The Power Figure

As leader of the Tory Opposition in the six years after the war,
Churchill made R. A. B. Butler his liaison officer with the
Lobby. I cannot remember a single occasion when Churchill
presented *himself* to Lobby meetings, which were less frequent
then than now and never openly referred to. R.A.B., on the other
hand, recognised the advantages and importance of the Lobby
and built up a strong relationship. He realised the possibilities
of a Lobby with a friendly disposition towards a heavily out-
numbered Conservative Opposition and was always ready to
discuss his party's policies and direction "on Lobby terms"
with us, individually or collectively.

Although this was the time when the Lobby comprised only
the "Nationals", some regional morning newspapers and the
B.B.C.—before the evening newspapers were admitted to swell
the Lobby ranks to about fifty—his special place with the correspondents earned him such regard that the majority of them
supported him when his chance came in 1963 to succeed
Harold Macmillan. His rejection through "Super Mac's"

devious drafting of Sir Alec Douglas-Home (then Lord Home) brought the Lobby's wrath down heavily on Macmillan and revealed undisguised sympathy for R.A.B. . . . always the Best Man but never the Groom. Another one on whom Winston Churchill relied heavily for his inside information on Press and party events was his aide and Chief Whip, Patrick Buchan-Hepburn. Patrick would occasionally meet us to present the Opposition's attitudes towards the business of the week ahead, or to give the occasional explanation why certain votes were being given a three-line whip (a mandatory instruction to an M.P. to attend a vote in the House).

Sir Anthony Eden

Third of the Premiers in chronological order was Sir Anthony Eden. He succeeded Churchill and, like him, kept away from the Lobby. By this time, however, the Lobby had increased in numbers and was undergoing modifications which amounted almost to a complete metamorphosis. The evening papers had been admitted and in a very short time the pattern and process of Lobby journalists' operations and practice had changed radically. Almost overnight the accreditations jumped to around fifty and this meant a much wider coverage of the M.P.s and the House's activities and a different style. At the same time, the day-to-day operations of the elected Chamber started taking different shape. Each successive government seemed to want to out-do its predecessor by increasing the legislative output.

This required more and more Standing Committees to take on work delegated to them from the Floor of the House. Since an important part of a Lobby Correspondent's job was to interpret Bills as they appeared, and to assess their impact, the Lobby became almost an integral part of the framework of both Government and Opposition activities. It was during Sir Anthony's period that I experienced my first Secret Session of Parliament.

A Secret Session is the only time the House of Commons is not open to public reporting. No record is kept by the Official Report (Hansard) of the proceedings, and it is a serious Breach of Parliamentary Privilege for anyone to break the rule of secrecy and attempt to report, as an authentic account of the proceedings, what has gone on behind the closed doors.

On this particular occasion the House of Commons had to be taken into the Prime Minister's confidence over the Six Days' War with Egypt which had been precipitated by President Nasser's take-over of the Suez Canal. That, and the aerial invasion by French and British paratroops, had aroused such indignation among M.P.s on all sides that Sir Anthony was forced to accede to a full-scale Commons debate. Security for the armed forces already involved, and the preparations for a return to a war footing in Britain only ten years after the end of the 1939/45 war, including troop movements in the Middle East, and also the refusal of the United States to back up the Eden policy, made such a debate in public quite impossible.

Sir Anthony used the only means open to him to meet the demand and yet withhold from the public vital information which could have jeopardised the whole Suez operation. He declared a Secret Session, something which is extremely rarely sought in our parliamentary scene since it is held to be contrary to our doctrine of democracy. It can, however, be effected very simply: all that is required is for any Member on the Floor of the House to ''Spy Strangers'' and the Chamber is cleared of all but elected Members. It was this debate, as I have revealed in Chapter 4, which brought me close to a Breach of Privilege which could easily have ended my Lobby career when it had hardly even begun. I have often wondered what would have happened had that report been published . . . It was a darned good story and, even if I *had* been barred from the House, I surely would have earned some fame as the chap who blew the gaff on Eden's débacle.

"Super Mac"

Harold Macmillan's succession to Sir Anthony Eden, who had been compelled to stand down because of serious abdominal afflictions, was a daunting rebuff of R. A. Butler's undoubted claim to the leadership. But the emergence of Harold Macmillan came after a superb period as Housing Minister—he tied his wagon to a seemingly impossible star, the promise to produce 500,000 houses for Britain's war-torn and inadequate housing-programme, and he delivered the goods; then he introduced the "can't lose gamble" of the £1 Premium Bond whilst Chancellor of the Exchequer. His was the charisma a flagging Tory party was seeking at the time and he justified their choice with his "You've never had it so good" image.

"Super Mac" was the title bestowed upon him by Vicky, the *Daily Mirror*'s brilliant political cartoonist, and he revelled in it. The original cartoon was bequeathed to the Press Gallery and today hangs in their dining room. Macmillan also restored to the House of Commons, by his Despatch Box appearances and speeches on the big days, a dignity and brilliance akin to the great Edwardian era. He was a true orator who had, and employed to the full, a mesmeric influence which seldom failed to hold even the most ebullient and explosive House. It was said of another orator Prime Minister, David Lloyd George, that he could charm the nightingales along the banks of the Severn; it can truly be said of Harold Macmillan that he was the last of the great House of Commons orators who could contain his opponents across the floor with his superb graciousness, his command and delivery of the spoken word.

He, too, made a practice of thinking up and employing at the right moment the "catchphrase". Like his contemporary, Nye Bevan, he had the knack of producing an apt and prophetic phrase which was bound to stick. After "You've never had it so good", perhaps the one which will continue to figure in public utterances for posterity is "A wind of change is blowing through Africa" ... How prophetic and accurate it turned out

'Super Mac' (The Rt. Hon. Harold Macmillan, M.P.).

to be. That wind grew stronger as independent nations sprang up across the continent and developed into the Third World.

Harold Macmillan also became a favourite with the Lobby and made a point of attending as many meetings as he could to maintain a personal contact. He always endeavoured to "look up" to the Lobby and our private meetings frequently ended in personal chats and reminiscences of his military and political experiences. Of the former there was one in particular which I recall because not long afterwards it was vouched for by a First World War colleague and fellow-Minister, Leader of the House of Commons, Harry Crookshank (later Lord Gainsborough).

It happened, we were told, during the British advance on the Somme during the First World War, when Harold Macmillan

was a young officer of the Grenadier Guards. On the road to
somewhere—not Damascus, he emphasised—they came under
heavy shell-fire. They dived for cover. Then, ''There was a
shambles and we suffered casualties. Suddenly, we heard a
voice from under some debris. We started digging. After a while
an arm appeared. Then the rest of the body appeared. It moved.
It muttered something . . . It turned out to be a Grenadier
Guards officer from another Battalion.''

Lieutenant Macmillan helped him out of the hole. ''I've been
there four days,'' explained the exhumed and exhausted officer.
''Welcome back, Lazarus,'' came the (typical) Macmillan
reply. From that day onwards Harry Crookshank, despite all
the various trappings of the high Ministerial Offices he held in
the post-second-war Tory governments, was always known
and referred to by his contemporaries as ''Lazarus''. The rescue
from the grave was the beginning of a comradeship which
brought both of them into politics with the Conservative Party.
They both reached the Front Bench, but it was the rescuer who
eventually went to the top.

The rapport between the Lobby and Prime Minister Harold
Macmillan was, up to that time in the post-war years, the most
stable and mutually successful ever. Lobby Correspondents had
always regarded among their privileges access to No. 10 when,
on big occasions, there was need of briefing from the top. It was
during the Macmillan régime that the practice was developed,
and with his encouragement, and that of Deputy Prime Minister R. A. B. Butler, who still maintained strong links with the
Lobby. Whereas the morning-paper correspondents, because of
their later deadlines, still preferred to carry out their duties in
the time-honoured fashion of Lobby trawls, the evening-paper
correspondents found the added facility of morning briefings at
No. 10, conducted by the P.M.'s Press liaison officers, a great
boon. In no time the practice of set Lobby briefings became an
integral part of the system, though it was still kept very much
under cover.

When it came to the choice of his successor, Macmillan caught out the political correspondents and even the Tory party itself, then in conference at Blackpool. With the Prime Minister in hospital in London, it was generally accepted that he would be announcing his retirement. But who was to follow him? And when would it be revealed? It was certainly not expected whilst the Party was in its annual assembly, with rumours and expectations rife. But, as he had done so many times previously, Super Mac fooled us all. Many of us had thought that, when it came, the choice would fall on R. A. B. Butler, then Deputy Prime Minister. It was to be his turn, many of us thought, and insofar as the professedly independent Lobby Correspondents were concerned, it would be a just and deserved promotion. Within the party, too, there was a large body of opinion which shared that view.

But R.A.B. was not the only contender, not by a long chalk. Whispers from London sources suggested that the then Foreign Secretary, Earl Home, was in touch with the Prime Minister in hospital and he had to be reckoned with as a surprise nomination. These triggered off another unexpected development. Into the ring went Viscount Hailsham's hat, and his intervention found support from many conference representatives. (Funny thing about the Conservative conferences. Whereas the other parties refer to their ''delegates'', the Tories prefer to call them ''representatives''.)

Now was the time for political pundits to study precedents. With two members of the House of Lords in the line-up, and the country not having had a Prime Minister in the House of Lords since the Marquis of Salisbury between 1885 and 1902, the majority thought the prize would go to R.A.B. But the robust and outspoken Hailsham was a popular figure with the rank-and-file Tories, who still held him in great esteem, if not awe, for his campanological performance at the Brighton Annual Conference two years earlier, when he sought to rally a dispirited party by seizing the chairman's bell to summon the faithful to greater efforts. "It rings for you, and you, and you . . ." he thundered from the platform, and, as if by magic, party spirits soared. His popularity resulted in Harold Macmillan's giving him the task of leading a government investigation into the economic and unemployment problems of the North-east.

It soon became apparent that the Rt. Hon. Viscount was ready to shed his title and revert to plain Mr Quintin Hogg (as indeed he did, a month later, to return to the House of Commons). As suddenly and as inexplicably as it had been thrown into the ring, the Hogg titfer was fished out again. We were at a loss about the reasoning, but later it was suggested that the grapevine between the Macmillan hospital bed and the conference platform had indicated the Prime Minister's decision hours before it was announced to the puzzled representatives. Momentarily R.A.B.'s star had burned brighter.

That evening, when the Earl Home arrived at Blackpool, as both the messenger from Macmillan and the victor, my colleagues and I received the news with stunned incredulity. It also made us feel extremely foolish for having almost unanimously opted for R.A.B. in our overnight stories! I can still remember the wan smile which greeted us when we caught up with him in the foyer of the hotel. That was the moment of truth for the man who had carried such a heavy Conservative Party burden through government and opposition periods. He acknowledged to some of us then that never again would he make a bid for the leadership. It was one of the saddest moments of my time in the Lobby.

Sir Alec Douglas-Home

Lord Home became Sir Alec Douglas-Home less than a week later. On disclaiming his title, and to enable him to take over as Prime Minister, the new session of Parliament which was due to be opened on October 29th was postponed to November 11th. On November 6th he was returned as M.P. for Kinross in a specially convened by-election.

He was the fifth post-war Prime Minister and I do not think he has ever denied that he became so less by his own choice and endeavours than because he was drafted precipitately by Macmillan who, worried by his own state of health, had thought it better to resolve any difficulty in the Party over his successor by making the appointment himself from his hospital bed. It fell to Sir Alec to lead the Conservatives into the 1964 General Election after being in office for only twelve months.

Two things can be laid on Sir Alec's shoulders for the loss of that election. The first was that he totally misread the mood of the country and in doing so committed the unpardonable sin of any Prime Minister by leaving the contest too late and himself without room for manoeuvre. The other was his unfortunate television image. Television played then what has been without doubt its most important role in the run-up to any election. The appearance on the screen of Sir Alec with his half-frame spectacles and his clipped accent drove a high proportion of the "uncommitted" voters into the Labour camp. Harold Wilson claimed that every party-political broadcast by Sir Alec was a bonus for Labour.

Sir Alec's credit-rating with the Lobby during his twelve months in Downing Street was not on a par with that of his predecessor, but he was always ready to meet the correspondents and discuss issues of the most controversial character. In general, though, the relationship was seldom more than 'lukewarm'.

One major difficulty was that Opposition leader, Harold Wilson, who had taken over the Labour leadership after the tragic death in January 1963 of Hugh Gaitskell, had become so tied in with the Lobby that he could virtually have claimed squatter's rights to our meetings. Like his former Front Bench colleague, Herbert Morrison, Harold Wilson was always available to the Lobby on request or without it. His "offerings" increased the Lobby's output considerably. Consequently the Labour Party, in the run-up to the election, enjoyed a greater prominence in the political stories generally. That was one time when the Labour Party could not complain about anti-socialist bias or lack of coverage as it so habitually does.

Harold Wilson

It would be foolish to claim it was a markedly pro-Labour or a massively anti-Tory bias which, in 1964, brought about the Conservatives' downfall by an overall Labour majority of five. Survival on that basis meant being constantly on the alert and winning and keeping as many friends and supporters as possible—and not only on the parliamentary benches. Harold Wilson knew how to employ the Lobby to his government's best advantage, and he held it in some respect even if not admiration. His first action on moving into No. 10 Downing Street had been to take, as his Chief Press Officer and adviser, Trevor (later Sir Trevor) Lloyd Hughes, Lobby Correspondent of the *Liverpool Daily Post*, who had been his Lobby man as M.P. for Huyton. Later he recruited another Lobby Correspondent, Joe Haines, to strengthen his Lobby liaison team.

Shrewd Harold retained his powerful personal connections with the Lobby and during his first period in government, between October 1964 and March 1966, seemed always to be available at its request. His tightrope majority, whittled down to three during the first eighteen months, had to be handled with extreme care, and the connections between the Lobby and Downing Street reached their strongest during that period. When, in 1966, the snap General Election brought the much-needed relief of a majority increased to ninetyseven overall, there was a marked change in the relationship.

During the previous eighteen months the Lobby had grown in status and authority with Downing Street, but there were squalls ahead and the Wilson régime thereafter saw periods of acute aggravation between the two. Accusations of leaks of advance information regarding government reports, White

Rt. Hon. Harold Wilson, M.P..

Papers and consultative documents, created, to put it mildly, a disturbed atmosphere. However, on balance, relationships between the political correspondents and Harold Wilson were as good as during any period in the post-war years. As Prime Minister he seemed always willing to accept invitations from the Lobby to meet its members. He also initiated what has since been sustained by successive Prime Ministers, namely a closer social association with No. 10. The sessional standing invitation for Lobby Correspondents and their wives to Downing Street is greatly appreciated and looked forward to. There was a marked difference in the Wilson approach to the Lobby system from that of his predecessors.

After the 1964 election he had promised One Hundred Days of Labour legislation. It was a rash promise, given in the first flush of victory. In fact the output of that Hundred Days was one solitary Act of Parliament which provided for concessionary fares for pensioners. This was because the government, with its majority of only three, was stifled and virtually in a strait-jacket so far as radical socialist reforms were concerned, election promises or not.

Things were different after the 1966 election. Wilson's major claim then was to launch Labour's programme for the future development of Britain's technical skills—and he did it first through the Lobby, during the Party's victory conference in Scarborough. I remember Lobby journalists receiving a briefing call from Trevor Lloyd Hughes, who promised the "hottest political story for years". A meeting was convened at the Albion Hotel and, unaware of what it was about or who would be there, we were greeted by the Prime Minister. It was obvious from the atmosphere that something big was happening. There was Harold Wilson, pipe in mouth, seated alongside the open hearth in the hotel lounge, bursting to confide in us the dynamic story we had been promised.

It was the most informal Lobby meeting with a member of government that I can recall, but it produced what had been promised. Harold Wilson's opening remarks were, "We're going to take Britain into the technological age," and he launched into a most comprehensive blueprint of technological development. Possibly it would have been more fitting to a session with industrial correspondents, but the implications, socially, economically, scientifically and in other ways, were so immense that it was better wrapped up as a political package. He had no briefs or written statements. He was for all the world like an over-indulged Cheshire Cat let loose.

He moved easily fron one aspect to the other and for the first time we noticed what was to become a byword in the Wilson era—his photographic and amazingly retentive mind, which allowed him to reel off dates and figures without a single reference note. "Harold the Memory Man" displayed all those skills that evening. It was something we were to see repeated many times at the Despatch Box in the Commons during his term of office. I still cannot satisfy my curiosity about it, but I was half convinced more than once that his off-the-cuff facility with dates and facts was a massive con-trick. It was certainly very impressive, though.

Harold Wilson was not a disciplinarian in the Attlee mould, but he could be pretty tough when occasion warranted. The history of the Labour Party has shown that tough leadership, even in some cases amounting to virtual dictatorship, is sometimes necessary to keep the Party on an even keel. Situations between centre, right and left, build up to fratricidal proportions over what one faction or other regards as a socialist dogma. It is then that the splits appear, and the leader has to exercise a sharp discipline to restore sanity to the ranks. There have been more instances of Labour M.P.s being expelled from their Parliamentary Party, or having the whip withdrawn, than in all the other Parties combined.

Another quality which distinguished Harold Wilson from his predecessors in the leadership was his wily patience in dealing with some of the more serious cases of rankers kicking over the traces, or with other disadvantageous situations. "A week is a long time in politics" was perhaps his most famous catchphrase. Another must surely be his observation, when cracking down on an upsurge of indiscipline within the Parliamentary Labour Party, that "Every dog is entitled to one bite".

Possibly the greatest Wilson miscalculation was the 1970 general election which he called "out of season". He went to the country in June in the expectation of another five-years' mandate based on Labour's proclaimed economic successes and bulky wage-packets. Indeed, early indications during the hectic three-weeks' campaigning suggested he had been right. But a Tory counter-attack based on industrial unrest caused by rising prices resulted in Ted Heath's being swept in with a majority of forty-three over Labour.

In this battle of fluctuating fortunes, the Lobby again played a prominent part, with its members having full and continuous access to the main contenders. Wilson conducted a Presidential -style campaign, spurring on the party workers. Ted Heath relied more on mass-meetings up and down the country. It was to be four years, however, before Harold Wilson was back at No. 10 Downing Street, and went on to complete what was, up to then, the longest Prime Ministerial peacetime stint for a century.

Ted Heath

Ted Heath, musician extraordinaire, sailor, bluff and jolly of countenance, was no stranger to Lobby Correspondents when he assumed the occupancy of No. 10 Downing Street. As leader of the Tory Opposition, he had been a pretty regular attender at our Commons businesss-meetings. Indeed, he was accepted almost as one of the family. He believed that personal contact with the Lobby was a necessary insurance for the time when he would be head of a Conservative government. His was perhaps

Interviewing 'Ted' Heath at No. 10, 1970.

the widest knowledge of the Lobby system of any Prime Minister because of his direct and very active contact with it as Government Chief Whip under both Sir Anthony Eden and Harold Macmillan.

However, relationships, though friendly enough, lacked much of the closer association which had developed during his predecessor's régime. Ted Heath decided that the ties with the Lobby would be better managed through Tory Central Office and the Civil Service avenues. The departure of the Lobby-experienced liaison officers of the No. 10 Press Office caused some problems to begin with, but things soon settled down.

There has never been any question that the Conservative Party organisation far excels that of the other parties, and not least in the dissemination of its Press-releases. The situation grew where the Lobby as a body was being fed with more stylised No. 10 handouts on government matters than hitherto. In turn it became the accepted thing that a great many of these handouts (which were not Tory Central Office party-briefs, I should point out) required explanation or elaboration by correspondents, and for this purpose it became necessary to have one or more meetings every day. Thus the process and system of true Lobby operations fell by the wayside.

The old method of face-to-face contacts in the Members' Lobby and around Westminster was being threatened by the handout system. Possibly there could be some excuse for correspondents accepting this hand-feeding operation as a routine due to the massive increase in the daily output and the pressures of the legislative sausage-machine that Westminster was becoming. Adding to the Lobby Correspondents' responsibilities was the extra involvement when Ted Heath took Britain into the Common Market.

Still, the twice-daily meetings with Lobby Correspondents at No. 10 were a welcomed means of keeping in direct touch with the government machine and this became the nub of operations. This in no way suggests, however, that Lobby Correspondents are the lackeys of *any* Administration. Press Office statements and briefings are never accepted as a simple routine way of getting the facts. They are, as they have always been, a basis for Lobby investigations and verification. Nothing is accepted at its face value, and this is as it should always be.

Clear in mind still is the situation which developed rapidly just before and after the Parliamentary Recess in 1973, when the first clues emerged that Ted Heath was contemplating an election. He wanted to challenge what he and several of his Ministers regarded as a move towards anarchy threatened by striking miners, especially the leftist element, and other trade union leaders. Resisting a government proposal to restrain spiralling wages, the miners had imposed an overtime ban which developed into an all-out strike with serious repercussions for industrial and domestic power supplies. A State of Emergency had been declared in November, but around Christmas the question emerging from No. 10 briefings with increasing frequency, indeed urgency, was "Who governs Britain?" It gained appeal as an election-winning ticket.

At that time it seemed the public were more sympathetic to the miners than to the government. But, as the New Year moved on, a slight shift in sympathies seemed to occur and a new political dimension was introduced. In two months public sympathy for the miners had eroded owing to more difficulties arising from fuel and power economies, and especially the strikers' obstinacy in standing out against a government they seemed ever more determined to bring down.

But the shift was too gradual for the government side. Lobby stories, most of them based on reports from the constituencies, urged caution on the Prime Minister. Ignoring also some of his closest advisers, Ted Heath decided the country had moved enough to his side and declared February 28th, 1974, as General Election day. The Conservative lost by five seats to Labour; the result was a hung Parliament which lasted seven months. The ironic fact, however, was that had he waited another fortnight, the outcome would undoubtedly have been different. It was one of the major miscalculations of that period, and a complete reversal of the June 1970 election which had brought Ted Heath into power on a result which had confounded all the pundits, and particularly the Opinion Polls. They had forecast a complete Labour victory and it seemed only one top-ranking Tory failed to be persuaded that a twelve per cent lead by Labour in the final stage of the campaign meant a Conservative defeat. That person was leader, Ted Heath. Ted was right then; they were wrong. Four years later the boot was on the other foot!

His decision to go to the country in February 1974, when the country was in the grip of the crippling miners' strike, was not made with the unanimous support of his Downing Street team. The platform, "Who governs Britain?", after three months of strike and mounting pay demands by the Unions, *might* have won him the election by a reasonable margin had the timing been right. Hindsight has since judged that in another two to three weeks the suffering British electorate would have responded. Although the strike was biting hard in February, public sympathy for the miners were still too strong. The wobbling voters needed just that extra time to go over to the Tories' side.

"If only Ted had listened . . ." was the accusing comment of some of his colleagues. I remember well the conversation I had with Jim Prior, then Leader of the House of Commons, only a day or so before the election declaration on 7th February, when he said that it was unlikely that the miners' leaders would allow any negotiation to call off the threatened all-out strike or allow other trade unions to negotiate other wage increases. In these circumstances he believed the situation as assessed by the Prime Minister would mean an election "before the end of March", or in any case later rather than sooner. He more or less repeated that view when he spoke at the Press Gallery Luncheon in the Commons on 6th February. His comments were that the government had gone as far as it felt it could to reach an agreement.

Pressures from with the Conservative Central Office and the party in the country, however, demanded an immediate and tough response from the leadership and it cost them the fight. It cost Ted Heath even more. He had to surrender his leadership to Margaret Thatcher who, six years later, created history by becoming Britain's first woman Prime Minister.

As a brilliant musician who would have won many accolades had he chosen that art as a career, Ted could have found consolation in his music. But, being the political animal he is, he has never given up hope that some day the Party will again require his leadership. This must be the most forlorn of hopes by now; even if Margaret Thatcher did have to be dispensed with, and neither I nor my colleagues at Westminster can see that happening. However, as has been said so often, "A week is a long time in politics".

Finally I have a personal thank-you to offer. It was in 1973, when the Conservatives were in conference at Blackpool, that I. was taken ill and confined to my bedroom with pneumonia. I was so ill that Frank Davenport, the hotel owner, sent for my wife. I missed the Heath winding-up speech and, as my colleagues were departing for London, I was lying in a semi-coma in my darkened hotel room. I became aware of movement and, as I turned my head, I saw an array of flowers floating through the open door. I was in such a state that I honestly thought I had passed on and I was seeing someone laying a floral tribute. Alone, and in the half light, I was resigned to my fate and dozed off.

When I was awakened shortly afterwards by my wife, the crisis having left me, I was shown a huge basket of flowers and fruit standing by the bed. In it was a note from Ted Heath, "Get well soon and join us. We'll miss you." Derek Howe, who was his Press Officer, and who had delivered the basket, told me later that the Prime Minister had shown much concern when he was told, after the Saturday winding-up, that I was pretty ill in my hotel. He had immediately ordered the get-well tribute and his gesture did more for my recovery than did the doctor's treatment.

Harold Wilson (2)

It was only after Ted Heath had been turned down by the Liberals, who spurned his offer to ally themselves with the Tories in forming a minority government, that Harold Wilson returned to his familiar surroundings in Downing Street. On that dank March day when the furniture-van pulled up outside No. 10, the Lobby was already buzzing with speculative stories about the length of his tenancy. During May and June he was subjected to incessant pleas from his own backbenches and the Party to go to the country again to resolve the stalemate in Parliament. He steadfastly refused, but the small majority suffered from the death of three Labour M.P.s, and when it reached two the inevitable happened. During the recess in September he named the date and in October the result was a Labour majority over the Tories of forty-three and an overall majority of three.

Thus Harold Wilson began his further term as Prime Minister, which lasted until March 1974. It was also his toughest period, for he was constantly at the mercy of the vagaries of the Liberal Dozen under the leadership of Jeremy Thorpe. But his manoeuvrings and adroitness in dealing with the Liberals without negotiating a Lib/Lab Pact kept the government going until his surprise resignation in March 1974.

This was another major event which caught the Lobby out. Although Harold Wilson is on record as having intimated to the Queen at least four months earlier that he would be retiring in March, before his 60th birthday, and had taken into confidence a few of his very closest friends, Lobby Correspondents did not have the slightest indication that the Prime Minister was preparing for his retirement from office. I could have scooped the pool on this but for the strict ethic of Lobby confidence, for I had received a clear hint of it at least a fortnight before it happened.

It was imparted to me quite innocently during a personal and private meeting with the Speaker, Mr. George Thomas. As very old friends we met from time to time in his private room in Mr. Speaker's House. On this particular morning we were discussing a feature interview and arranging for some impromptu photographs to be taken on the Terrace. I remember our conversation turned to Mrs Mary Wilson and her poetry, and an autographed copy he had procured for my wife. Apropos of nothing in particular, George mentioned something about how strange it would be when Harold went ... ''When?'' I enquired, because there was no question in any backbench gossip of the Prime Minister standing down. George looked me straight in the eye, pursed his lips, said he should never have mentioned it and then added, ''Don't forget, Davey (he called me that sometimes when he was imparting something special and private), this is strictly on Lobby terms.''

He never referred to it again, neither before nor after the resignation announcement. But he knew I would not have betrayed his confidence even if he had given me the date—which he couldn't then. Later, when Harold made his resignation statement to the House, he confirmed he had communicated with Mr Speaker some months before.

After that meeting I could have written a speculative piece about the Wilson future, but there was nothing to back it up in the weekly trawl. However, in my weekly chat with my Editor about the political scene I did refer to a possible Wilson resignation. In the absence of any clear-cut reaction from either of us, the matter was not pursued. But when it happened he reminded me of that conversation. I never revealed how it had come about. Our contacts with Ministers and M.P.s were strictly personal and not something one discussed outside our

circle. That has been the strength and the mystique of the
Lobby and its system.

There were few occasions when I had, or sought to have,
personal meetings with Harold Wilson as Prime Minister, but
as someone who always showed the greatest interest in, and
regard for, the Principality, he was always helpful through his
personal staff at No. 10 Downing Street whenever I sought his
support as Welsh Lobby Correspondent. I shall forever be grateful to him for the typical, homely and generous, gesture he
made when our daughter, Marilyn, was married to John Rowe
in Ickenham, Middlesex. We had invited both George Thomas,
then Secretary of State for Wales, and John Morris, Defence
Minister for Procurement, to the wedding. George had told
Harold about it and the Prime Minister graciously sent a
personal message to wish the happy couple the very best in life.
It made their day . . . and my wife's and mine too.

Harold Wilson's last period in office was an eventful one for
Wales in at least two respects. Firstly, the long-promised effort
to bring a measure of Home Rule to Wales (and Scotland) was
attempted for the first time by a Socialist government. Second-
ly, his retirement halfway through the parliamentary session
enabled a Welsh M.P., for the second time in history, to become
Prime Minister. Well, it was a demi-glory for Wales because his
successor, Leonard James Callaghan, elected a Cardiff M.P. in
1945, was not actually Welsh, though he claimed ''naturalis-
ation'' by virtue of more than forty years' involvement in
Welsh affairs.

Failure to get his Wales Devolution Bill onto the Statute
Book was one of Harold Wilson's biggest political disappointments. He had hoped to go out in a blaze of glory with an
emancipated Principality—and a greater measure of devolution
for Scotland—among his major achievements. It was a bitter
pill when the measure was rejected not only by Parliament,
with many Labour M.P.'s resolutely opposed to and voting
against the Bill, if not the principle, but the Welsh people also

cast it out in the notable referendum of March 1st (St. David's Day) 1979.

The Parliamentary reversal was not a factor in Wilson's retirement. As he had confessed before the first impasse, he had decided to go within two years of the 1974 election in any case. The Devolution issue, however, was the hottest legacy left to Jim Callaghan on his succession, and it was the one which ultimately caused his downfall.

During the early skirmishes over devolution, Harold Wilson failed to inject the Lobby with any great enthusiasm for the issue. The exceptions were myself, David Rose of the *Liverpool Daily Post*, and our Scottish colleagues. For the rest of our colleagues the running story—it went on for two years after the White Paper embodying the Kilbradon/Hunt Royal Commission recommendations had been published—was concerned more with splits in the Labour Party over the proposals for separate Welsh and Scottish Assemblies, and the role of backbencher, Neil Kinnock, then M.P. for Bedwellty, the rebel leading a Welsh splinter-group.

It was left to Jim Callaghan to lay the creature to rest after the four-to-one rejection in the Welsh referendum and Scotland's failure to secure a 40 percent pro-devolution vote.

Leonard James Callaghan

Leonard James Callaghan was one of the trio of Cardiff M.P.s to enter the House in 1945. The others were George Thomas—now Viscount Tonypandy, but still the same old George to one of the widest circle of friends any man could hope for—and Hilary Marquand, all Labour.

When I entered the House he already, after one year, had his feet firmly placed on the first rung of the ladder which ultimately led to the Premiership. Jim was Parliamentary Secretary at the Ministry of Transport and already earmarked by Clement Attlee, and judged by the more astute among the

Lobby correspondents, as an up-and-coming figure. He has achieved his ambition, and his memoirs will undoubtedly reflect on those early days. But Jim's account will not contain those memoirs that I shall recount here.

As he was one of my Welsh band of M.P.s it was only natural that I should pay particular attention to his achievements, and it was through him that I became involved early on in an issue of particular interest and importance to South Wales. The Severn Bridge project had been long mooted, but no government had considered it necessary, or viable, before the war. The Attlee government, however, had included it in a wide-ranging industrial development for South Wales as the road-bridge link with England, and especially the Port of Bristol. It had therefore become a major issue.

About the beginning of 1947 the project had been added to the Attlee Cabinet's list of major construction and reconstruction plans and Alf Barnes, Minister of Transport, became involved in plans which had been submitted by a firm of Cardiff architects. Without making any elaborate disclosures, Jim Callaghan helped me to keep on the right lines from time to time about the Severn Bridge.

There were times when I was on the verge of writing that the government had agreed to include the programme in its five-year plan for post-war development. The Ministry were keen to give the impression that everything was ready and that the Marshal Aid cash from the Americans would enable the project to go ahead in the early fifties. It was only Jim's guidance and honest appraisal which kept me from committing myself too soon to this major story which I was so desperately anxious to write. It would have been a feather in my cap . . . if it had been right! As it happened, he saved me from making a fool of myself and deluding Welsh industrialists who were anxiously watching for signs of a go-ahead. For this I shall always be grateful to him.

At that time, as I recall, the Severn Bridge would have cost around £7 million. It had to be abandoned, along with several other projects, because of the lack of cash. When, eventually, it did receive the go-ahead and work on it began, the original estimate had been more than doubled. Before it was completed, that figure had been more than quadrupled.

Our association in the Lobby, though pleasant enough in appearance, was never on par with that of others of Jim's colleagues, and for years it has rankled in my mind that this may have been due to something which has stuck in my craw for all those years. In those early years M.P.s were not anywhere near highly paid. This meant that for many backbenchers, whose salary was around £600 a year, and who had families to support, there had to be a supplementary income if they were to have a reasonable standard of living. There was no such thing as London-weighting, and the expense of keeping virtually two homes going when Members had to put in four and five days a week at Westminster was pretty crippling.

The lot of backbench M.P. then was very different from that of the, by comparison, cossetted M.P. today. Except for the M.P.'s fare to and from the constituency and the House of Commons, paid expenses were virtually non-existent. There was no financial help for secretarial and research costs and it behoved the M.P. dependent on his parliamentary pay to seek out another source of income. Most of them who were able offered their services to the media (which consisted of B.B.C. radio and the newspapers or journals, national and local).

And so it happened that Jim Callaghan, one of the ablest of his intake, and with more than five years' Ministerial experience, was invited to contribute a weekly parliamentary political column to a Sunday newspaper whose political leanings were somewhat left of centre. He had reverted to the back-benches after the 1951 Attlee election defeat and obviously the income from the extra source would be welcomed by a married man with a young family. In the Press Gallery one day I received a call from Jim asking me to meet him outside the Members' Library. I found him waiting for me at the high desk at the beginning of the corridor leading to the Members' Lobby and sensed a kind of embarrassment as he opened the conversation.

It is true to say that Jim Callaghan had always been very circumspect insofar as his dealings with the Lobby and myself were concerned. He was regarded by many of us at the time as an introvert, a strange attitude for an M.P. He seldom asked for or seemed to expect any reciprocal favours, which is why the reason for our meeting rather surprised me. He explained that the offer of a Sunday column was conditional upon his being a member of the National Union of Journalists. Would I be prepared to propose him for membership? I had no reason to doubt that Jim was a competent writer and would do the job better than most of his M.P. colleagues who were similarly placed, but that was not the point.

At that time the unemployment rate among journalists was pretty high, especially in Fleet Street. My immediate reaction to the request was that, on principle, I could not support it. To belong to the N.U.J. one had to be a bona fide journalist. Jim was not. He was a professional politician. To my mind, if he were to be proposed and accepted he might be depriving a fellow-journalist of a job. On this basis I turned down his request. He took it very well, and the matter was never again raised between us, but the feeling persisted with me that that brief meeting greatly altered the relationship between us. In retrospect I came to accept that my decision had been wrong. Many M.P.s became columnists as a secondary vocation and made a success of it. Some are still at it, having long departed the Westminster scene. But who knows that my rejection was not a blessing in disguise for Jim. Had he taken seriously to journalism the fates might have decreed the road to Fleet Street instead of to No. 10 Downing Street, via the Treasury, the Foreign Office and the Home Office. I cannot say whether Jim thought any more of the matter after being turned down. I know I have, many times.

The next eight years passed without any incident of note between Jim Callaghan and myself. We were on the usual Lobby/back-bencher terms, and he was yet to figure much in the limelight, although he had been making steady progress through the Party ranks. Then came the 1959 General Election.

The future Prime Minister went into it without any question in his own mind that he was certain to be re-elected. His majority in the previous (1955) election had been 3,240, and the Cardiff South-East seat was regarded by Labour as safe. There was every reason for assuming so, because the incumbent was already regarded as one of the up-and-coming Labour M.P.'s However, there was to be a shock for Jim and the Labour Party, and I'm afraid I had to carry the blame for many years afterwards. Until now the why's and the wherefore's have never been revealed.

As the result of an eve-of-poll "revelation" in the *Western Mail* the Labour vote plummeted and Jim's majority crashed to 868, bringing it well within the risk that this Cardiff seat might be lost to the Conservatives at the next election. What happened was this.

For twelve years it had been my practice to tour Wales during the four-weeks' General Election campaigns, giving special attention to those seats where a change was probable or even possible. Cardiff South-East was not on my list in 1959. Again, as in previous campaigns, I was due to wind up my tour in Cardiff on Polling Day. I would remain at the office for the results and deal with the election story as the national scene unfolded between midnight and five a.m.

A few days before the wind-up of my tour I was surprised to receive a personal call from the Hon. Anthony Berry, then Managing Editor of the *Western Mail.* He suggested I change my itinerary and come to Cardiff a couple of days earlier. Not for me to question why! He was the boss and for some reason he wanted me near to hand ... as I thought. Consequently I skipped a few constituencies and turned up at the office two days before scheduled. Even then I was not told the reason for the change.

First glimmer of what was afoot came when I was asked to make a special enquiry into the voting prospects in Cardiff South-East. It was being fought for the Conservatives by Michael Roberts, then a local schoolmaster, who had made a strong impression when he stood against Callaghan in the 1955 General Election. Michael's agent was G. V. Wynne Jones ("Geevers" to everyone in Cardiff and throughout sporting circles in and beyond Wales by virtue of his status as a radio commentator for major sporting events, particularly International Rugby matches at Cardiff Arms Park).

Undoubtedly there was a strong underlying fear in the constituency about the future of jobs in the local steelworks, the mainstay of employment for a powerful section of the division's voters. The steel industry had been denationalised by an earlier Conservative government and one of the pledges in Labour's election manifesto was a return to public ownership of all the major sections of the industry. The suggestion was being firmly implanted among the steelworkers and their families in the Roath, Adamstown and Splott areas and part of Penarth, that the return of a Labour government and re-nationalisation would result in some closures and the loss of jobs.

Wages in the steelworks were good and it was said that a high percentage of the workers and their families were heavily committed to hire purchases. The inference was that to vote Labour would put all these at risk. This was the construction many workers put on a letter from the management of Guest, Keen and Nettlefolds, the biggest employer, which urged workers and their families to withstand the Labour threat to their increasingly high standard of living; and this was the keynote of Mike Roberts's campaign, skilfully managed by "Geevers" in conjunction with the works management.

It was my function to bring out in my report—which was a factual account of my two days' investigation into voters' reactions, and which really did show substantial concern—the Conservatives' warning. Tony Berry showed me the letter which had been circulated, so I was not being asked to pluck any anti-Labour propaganda out of thin air. It already existed. This had nothing to do with me, but was a matter for the editors. The Tory plot, for that is what it was, was to run the story on the eve-of-poll. In this way the local Labour party would not have the opportunity of replying which it would have demanded if the story had been published earlier.

It was a coup which nearly came off. A secret opinion-poll of the constituency conducted virtually at the very last moment showed the distinct possibility that Jim Callaghan would be defeated. Labour and Conservatives were neck-and-neck, with the other parties nowhere. That evening Tony Berry's office was buzzing like a beehive and I was being called in from time to time to be told that all the signs were that the Callaghan citadel was falling.

Tony Berry's commitment had been total and the article had been given much prominence. Of course, he had ambitions to enter Parliament himself one day—and he did later with tragic consequences—but this was his first major plunge into politics. Little did one realise then that not only would he reach the House of Commons but he would become a Comptroller of the Royal Household, a Whip with close connections with and access to Prime Minister Margaret Thatcher, and receive a Knighthood. Nor could one have foreseen the terrible tragedy twenty-five years on when he would be a victim of the terrorist attack on the Grand Hotel, Brighton, during the 1984 Conservative Party Conference.

However, the outcome of the 1959 plot was that Jim Callaghan was returned with a meagre 868 majority. I could not be at the count that night because I had to stay at the office to monitor national results, but I was told by a colleague of the drama enacted there. The word had gone around and everyone's eyes were on Jim and his wife, Audrey, as the count proceeded. Judging by their expressions it looked as though the steelworkers' traditional support had dwindled sensationally to let Mike Roberts in and that Jim was accepting it. But the Labour loyalists held on.

When the result reached the Managing Editor's office the disappointment was allayed only slightly by the large drop in Labour's majority. Personally I was not politically involved or affected. I had my own job to do in assessing, to the best of my professional ability, what would be the likely outcome of the Cardiff South-East campaign. The result vindicated that judgement. I soon realised, however, that I was being blamed by the Labour camp for what had happened, and they went on blaming me for many years. Even in 1970, when I was submitted for the C.B.E., I gathered from an unimpeachable source that the happenings eleven years earlier had figured in the reckoning. To the professed amazement of the then Secretary of State for Wales, Peter Thomas, Q.C., I appeared among the M.B.E.'s.

Jim Callaghan's succession to the Premiership on 5th April, 1976, had been secured after a ten days' cliff-hanging operation within the Parliamentary Labour Party for the election of a new leader. At that time Cledwyn Hughes (now Lord Cledwyn of Penrhos) was Chairman of the Parliamentary Party. He was a stickler for protocol and procedure and I recall that many times during Lobby briefings after Parliamentary Party meetings we would indulge in brief backchats in Welsh. Sometimes in this way, but only seldom, I was able to get the edge on my colleagues about the story behind the briefing.

During the leadership voting, about which I was particularly concerned because two of my Welsh M.P.s were front-runners, Jim and Michael Foot, I tried desperately hard to get Cledwyn to feed me with a little more than the rest. But no, there was nothing doing. We had a friendly relationship and his reticence about giving a little more about the inside story on likely voting trends did not affect this. Naturally I felt a little peeved at times and formed the opinion that Cledwyn was a Foot rather than a

Callaghan man. Three ballots were necessary before Jim
Callaghan emerged the winner. On the first, Michael had a lead
of six votes, but this was not conclusive. In the final ballot Jim
got 176 votes to Michael's 137.

Whatever Cledwyn's real feelings were during the leadership
battle, as soon as Jim had got hold of the reins and was showing
himself to be a surprisingly tough leader, as was required in the
circumstances, it became patently clear that the two of them
were closer than, to my knowledge, they had ever been.
Cledwyn, as Parliamentary Party Chairman, held considerable
power in the ranks. Jim, on the other hand, was only too well
aware of the problems of keeping the government going in the
face of widening splits. The Devolution issue was blowing wide
open and nearing its climax. The Tories were snapping at the
government's heels, sensing that internal problems were
weaking the structure, and seeking to force another election on
the question of the widening incomes-and-prices crisis.

In the face of this, Jim sought the only escape-route open to
him, a pact with the Liberals. And it was Cledwyn who was
deputed to make the overtures, and who succeeded in bringing
Callaghan and Steel, the Liberal leader, together. It in no way
demeans the skilled handling of the situation by Cledwyn
Hughes, or belittles his achievements, to say that Lobby
opinion at that time was that Jim would be knocking at an open
Liberal door if he was peddling a Lib/Lab pact. The Liberals
were desperately keen themselves to stave off a late 1977 or
early 1978 General Election. Although David Steel argued
publicly that it was the Liberals' aim and intention to allow
the new leadership in government the opportunity to settle
the prices-and-incomes crisis, and especially the worsening
relationships with the trade unions, privately it was admitted
that an early General Election forced by the Conservatives
would be the worst possible thing for the Liberals, whose
fortunes at that time were at a low ebb. This was not contested
by David Steel when he met the Lobby in his room at the House

almost within minutes of the official Lib/Lab pact announcement. I was there.

The deed done, it saw the Callaghan government through that dreadful winter of discontent and into March 1978. They were months when the Lobby was assiduously courted from No. 10 Downing Street, with Tom (now Sir Tom) MacCaffrey burning more midnight oil, and wearing out more shoe-leather than any of his predecessors along the well-trodden paths between Downing Street and the Lobby room on the top floor of the Palace of Westminster.

Jim Callaghan's sojourn was a remarkable feat of political discretion and manoeuvrability, and it might have lasted longer than it did, except for one thing. Ironically, it was the people of his adopted land who ultimately brought it all to an end. The referendum he had allowed on the Devolution issue, and which Plaid Cymru (The Welsh Nationalist Party) had dubbed ''the shameful and iniquitous betrayal of Welsh national aspirations'' brought defeat in the House for Callaghan.

As Harold Wilson commented some years later, ''If for a time it was rotten garbage (a legacy of the unions' rebellion against continuing wage-restraints) that threatened the Labour government, it was Devolution which forced it to go to the country''; and to the defeat which ushered in the Saga of the Iron Maiden. Callaghan was finally scuppered by one vote in a Tory-sponsored Motion of No Confidence over Devolution, with his Lib/Lab Pact scuttled and dozens of his own back-benchers in revolt.

More than that, and with another ironic twist of political fortune, it can be said that that event laid the path from the back-benches to the party leadership for another Welsh M.P. and the possibility of Wales producing its third Prime Minister in this century. Neil Kinnock was one of six Welsh Labour M.P.'s who rebelled against the Welsh Assembly proposal. The other five quickly acknowledged his leadership and the qualities he developed in that difficult situation have served him well.

It was only to be expected when he announced early in 1987

that he would not be contesting the next General Election that Jim Callahan, then Father of the House, would have further recognition given to him for an illustrous political and public service career.

He was, and still is entitled to elevation to the House of Lords as a past Prime Minister. But those who know him closest had no reason to believe that on retirement from the House of Commons he would advance his claim to the entitlement which could have brought him an Earldom.

Instead, the recognition, so amply and justly earned and deserved, came directly from Her Majesty. In conferring upon him the Knighthood of the Garter, the Honour solely within the Queen's own giving, and before he relinquished his membership of the Commons, the Sovereign reflected the opinion of all sides of the House of Commons, and indeed of the country, irrespective of political allegiances.

It was for Sir James—and of course Lady Audrey—the most deserved insignia of merit.

Only a few weeks before the Knighthood was gazetted we had met in the Committee corridor at the House of Commons and discussed briefly his memoirs and their publication. I recall hinting at a possible announcement of an elevation to The Other Place, by which the House of Lords is commonly referred to in the Lower Chamber. It received a shake of the head, and that enigmatic smile and drawl . . . "come, come David."

In retrospect I wonder whether the conferment of the K.G., the most coveted of the Sovereign's personal accolade, had already been signified and if, once again, he had wondered whether my casual enquiry was just another Lobby guile.

But the secret had been too well kept. The Palace announcement in due course took us all by surprise, but only to the extent that no prior hint had been forthcoming.

Along with a host of others of his contemporaries in a lifetime of Parliamentary service, I add my congratulations to Sir James, K.G.

Margaret Thatcher

Mrs. Thatcher made political history by becoming the first woman ever elected leader of the Conservative Party. That was in February, 1975. It was an inspirational breakthrough which soon brought its reward, because she led the Party to victory in the first election under her command, in 1979.

For the four years she was Leader of the Opposition, Margaret Thatcher paid handsome court to the Lobby. In those days she was anything but the Iron Maiden, a title with which the Soviets branded her later and with every justification as a tough negotiator. We knew her as a demure damsel whose co-operation and genuine anxiety to be helpful quickly overcame the chauvinistic suspicions of those of us who were accustomed to more forthright male contacts. From the beginning, however, she made it clear that she did not wish to be treated differently.

It wasn't only that she employed her undoubted charm to get onto the same wavelength as the Lobby, she soon made it apparent, with her winning smile and her penchant for using christian names when addressing an individual, that she also had wit and the ability to get her brief across with conviction. This was something new for all of us and any misgivings that might have been felt at the beginning soon evaporated.

As Opposition Leader she made it her duty to take the weekly meetings which had long been an established part of the liaison between the Lobby and the main Parties. In fact Margaret Thatcher turned out to be the most efficient in a long line of predecessors. During this period, and in the years following, I never felt that she was deliberately using Lobby Correspondents to secure a wider dissemination of Tory views than was gained by the other Parties. In retrospect I can accept that her training as a lawyer and her Ministerial experience in two Conservative governments, coupled with the fact that we were dealing for the first time with a woman who, even then, was unique in politics, were the main ingredients for her success. And by gosh she was good at getting her cases across!

All pals together: Rt. Hon. Margaret Thatcher, M.P. with Press Gallery and Lobby Correspondents, 1979.

This was a good training-ground for her future and helped with the acquisition of a toughness in leadership which has amounted almost to ruthlessness in getting her political way. However, Mrs. Thatcher, Prime Minister, has moved away from the institution of the Lobby. The Thatcher view and influence have long been fed back through the sharply honed and meticulously efficient Press Office at No. 10 Downing Street, for which she has the highest regard and on which she depends greatly. But it might have served her and the government better in awkward situations such as the Westland Affair, and the occasional embarrassing leaks, to have repaired her fences with those who were so close and useful in the days of yore, and herself sought to put some records straight in the old, traditional, style. It's what Harold Wilson would have done!

Of course, it is a different ball game being at the head of a government than operating in the clinically critical fashion of a Leader of the Opposition where a persistent and all-out attack on the opponents' policies are an essential and very necessary function.

With two successful elections under her belt and with an unquenchable ambition to be the first Prime Minister in this century to make it three in a row, her choice of June 11th for that momentous challenge was not a lightly taken decision.

Indeed, many of us in the Lobby, exercising that sixth sense which has been attributed to us in dealing with major decisions, forecast even before the Christmas 1986 recess that June would be the most favoured choice for her vital election.

So many things pointed to the mid-year election; such as the increasingly favourable economic forecasts, the lower taxation predictions (confirmed in the following budget), the presentation of lower unemployment trends and a carefully managed programme of summit meetings including those in Washington, Moscow and Venice. There were also the tours of the Eruopean Community capitals, most of which were made known to the Lobby well in advance of their happening. But perhaps more than anything else in the judgement of my colleagues and myself which influenced the predictions of a June election was that Mrs Thatcher is a creature of habit.

She had led her party to victory in June 1983 on virtually the same programme and it was again being quietly groomed for the challenge ahead. Since she had been successful then there was little or no doubt in her mind that it would be so again. Maggie does not think in terms of failure!

I have to confess to one further clue which had been given to me personally relating to the probability of a June election. I had been asked whether I would be away on holiday, or whatever, during that time as far back as November 1986. The probability was that I would not be (which proved to be wrong in any case) and on this assumption I was again invited, unattached as I am these days to any particular publication, to join the team of political writers which is recruited by the Conservative Central Office organisation during general elections for the purpose of feature articles on policy issues. I had served on the team in 1983. The fresh invitation hardened my speculation from the possible to the probable on the election date.

With the Labour Party mounting its challenge under a virtually untested leader, and the Tory party machine even then being geared to its most efficient operational standard ever, it seemed logical that, short of a major economic crisis, the portents suggested success in June rather than for hanging on later.

So it proved. And the overwhelming victory of a hundred plus majority once again emphasised the charismatic influences which Margaret Thatcher had so markedly sustained during her eight years' Premiership not only within her own party but also on the fringes. The outcome was an endorsement of national support for Thatcherism.

For the next four years at least she could rule supreme over the Conservative Party and Britain for there seemed to be no-one at the time who could be offered as a likely challenger to her leadership. Her tenacity in facing up to a third parliament—''and on, and on, and on . . .'' she had declared during a public interview—was yet another indication of her determination to see through her further and far-reaching plan to uproot socialism in Britain.

The other likely threat to Thatcherism (which had now become an accepted expression for posterity), namely The Alliance—of the S.D.P. and Liberal parties—which had failed so dismally in the election, had yet to be dealt with. The certainty, however, was that the Saga of Maggie was a very long way from being ended.

Chapter 17: Neil Kinnock . . . Still Future Prime Minister?

Should it have been that the electorate had denied Margaret Thatcher her third successive period in office, history would have recorded a meteoric rise for a young Bedwellty trade union tutor, from back bencher to Prime Minister within seventeen years.

Neil Kinnock's fierce but unavailing first time challenge for the key to No. 10 Downing Street, and the return of a Labour government after eight years in Opposition, projected the passionate ambition which had guided his progress to the leadership of the Labour Party at the age of forty four.

He was two years younger than was Harold Wilson when he became leader of the party, and he had outstripped his contemporaries and the then rising stars in the Labour Party of the sixties. The Premiership was the goal young Neil Kinnock set himself the day he resigned as Parliamentary Private Secretary to Michael Foot in 1975. But that his first tilt should have come within twelve years of that occurrence could only have been a considerable and warming surprise for him.

'Neil' on the Terrace (Neil Kinnock, M.P. with—left to right: Rt. Hon. Merlyn Rees, M.P.; Lord Davies of Rhondda; Max Boyce; the Author).

That he failed to make it then in no way dampened the fires of ambition. Neil knew there would be another bite at the cherry, and he was both young enough, and dedicated to the task, to await the next time round. For the immediate future, however, what would be taxing his nerve most had to be the longer term reverberations within the Labour Pary of that electoral defeat.

On whom would the burden of defeat rest as the party inquests over the next few months—and perhaps even years—sought to establish the cause and responsibility for that defeat? One thing which emerged clearly from the election campaign was that Neil Kinnock led his party from the front and from the outset. He proved his capability as a leader in the measure of control he exercised over the internal warring factions, and particularly the militants' criticisms of the party programme as lacking in ''true socialist content''. It was Labour's policy, not the man to implement it, that the electorate rejected.

And so the question must remain an open one; is there still the prospect of a third Welsh Member of Parliament becoming Prime Minister in this century? Neil Kinnock was elected M.P. for Bedwellty in June 1970 following the retirement of my old friend Harold (later Sir Harold) Finch. There was little at the time to suggest his rapid rise to the leadership of the Labour Party in 1985, and with the prospect of leading a fourth post war Socialist government. To me his astonishing race to the top has been the more remarkable because it all happened after his first step in 1975.

Let me explain: Neil showed nothing outstanding among the 1970 General Election intake, but he learned the ways of the House of Commons very quickly. He trod the by-ways very tactfully, taking care not to be embroiled with any of the controversial groups with which the Parliamentary Labour Party was littered at that time.

He was, however, an effervescent character, sharp and witty, and with a pleasant and infectious smile and a Welsh lilt which was a dead giveaway when indulging, as he often did, in lively arguments in the Lobby or the Tea-Room or on the Terrace with his own colleagues or anyone who was prepared to exchange quips, quotes or contentions. Where Rugby was concerned, there was no more fervent contender.

Strangely enough, I can never recall him losing his temper in the view or hearing of friends or others, though I remember thinking, shortly after we met in the House, that here was someone I would have to handle with care . . . but only because he was a "cochyn" (ginger-haired).

As the months rolled on and his interests increased in questions and debates (especially in the fields of education and the mining industry), we became good friends. Nye Bevan had been his idol and I recall some of our chats in the Strangers Tea-Room and on the Terrace over pots of tea, when he expressed his regret that the great man had left the scene before he, Neil, had made it to the Commons. But he still basked in the Bevan aura through his strong friendship with Michael Foot, who had adopted the mantle of Bevan as his successor at Ebbw Vale, the constituency near to Bedwellty. Foot was already established by then as Nye's biographer.

In less than four years on the backbenches Neil mounted what must have seemed to him then the first rung of the ladder: he accepted the job of Parliamentary Private Secretary to Michael Foot, then Secretary of State for Employment. This was the most challenging Department of the Wilson government and Neil must have had aspirations that ere long he would be treading the path to the Ministerial Bench under the tutelage of one of the most powerful of Labour's Ministers. As has so often happened when an ambitious backbencher takes up this apprenticeship, it did not take young Neil long to realise he was the victim of a strait-jacket.

Freedom in the House is the first casualty of this particular office. A "P.P.S." becomes strangled in a network of prohibitions. He cannot stand up in the House and express himself on any matters which directly involve the Department or the office of the Minister. Outside the House the same conditions apply. It is a penalty which many are prepared to accept for the ''glory'' of serving a particular Minister, and in the hope that loyalty will bring its own reward and recognition.

The title has a sort of grandiloquence which gives the impression that its holder has a position of substance in government administration. It isn't so. It has been more rightly described as a fetch-and-carry function, a kind of fagging system which must be available to every Minister. Perhaps the most important aspect of the job is that the P.P.S. has to be the channel between the Minister and the grapevines, within the House and along Whitehall, which carry all the gossip and worthwhile information through those corridors of power. A good P.P.S. must be the possessor of a delicate ear to catch the gossip, and an acute sense to evaluate the strengths or weaknesses of movements, particularly where they are directed towards his boss. All in all, one might say, a most demanding and sometimes unpopular job, but the experience it brings is regarded as worth all its restrictions—except, of course, the one which keeps an ambitious M.P. mum!

The significance of what I called his ''1975 step'' was that, after just over a year as Michael's P.P.S., Neil must have started thinking earnestly whether his state of suspended animation, insofar as his backbench contributions were concerned, was having an adverse effect on his future rather than enhancing his promotion prospects. I thought this was so when we were walking down the Committee Corridor after a Welsh Labour Group meeting and he raised with me the subject of his likely resignation from the post. I sensed it was an exploratory discussion. After all, it was no new thing for an M.P. to raise with his Lobby Correspondent, in confidence, probable intentions so that he might secure either advice or some kind of reaction.

It wasn't that he was fed up with the job, he was disappointed that he could not take a more active part in many of the debates on the Floor of the House. He hadn't been getting publicity either, and that, as I remember being mentioned in our conversation, could be the most important factor. Up cropped that old saying of his early mentor again, "It doesn't matter what they say about you so long as they say something." It hadn't mattered to Nye that he classified the Fourth Estate as being "lower than vermin".

It would be presumptuous in the extreme to claim that Neil acted on any advice from me, but I do believe our conversation was what finally pushed him to the edge of resignation as P.P.S. We were walking down the back-stairs to the Members' Tea-Room when he remarked, "I'll give it some more thought and as soon as I make up my mind, you'll be the first to know." It wasn't more than a couple of hours later that I got his telephone-call. He simply said, "I've packed it in." What had Michael said about it? "We've parted the best of friends. Nothing to do with personalities," he answered. A sense of relief came through clearly in the rest of the conversation. That night I wrote a piece announcing the resignation. I wish I had added, "Neil Kinnock is on his way to the top", which was true because, freed from his backbench inhibitions and prohibitions, he became a distinctive character. Four years later he made the Front Bench, but it was as Education Spokesman for the Opposition against the first Thatcher government. He had been in the House of Commons nine years.

After casting off his P.P.S. role, Neil had set out with determination to establish himself as one of the bright young men in Labour's ranks. There was the need to clutch at something which would give him the attention and experience of leadership. It came in the shape of the hottest political chestnut since the war, and it involved him both as a politician and a Welshman. Devolution for Wales (and Scotland) was the issue on which he took a courageous and, party-wise, a minority stand. He became the Labour-Party-loyalist-turned-rebel just as his hero, Nye Bevan, had done with his Bevanite Group nearly twenty years earlier.

Harold Wilson had included in his Parliamentary programme for the 1968 session a Royal Commission on Devolution for Scotland and Wales. As Parliament waited on the recommendations, the principle of which carried overwhelming support within the Labour Party, small segments formed opposing movements. The great debate got under way with one faction supporting the idea of Home Rule and a total severance from Westminster of all administrative controls, another urging no more than a controlled devolution of Westminster responsibilities, and yet another demanding the retention of status quo. It was a mess of confusion.

The Royal Commission reported in October 1971. By this time lines had been clearly drawn between the opposing factions at Westminster and in the country. The Commission rejected self-government for Wales, but suggested, as a compromise, the establishment of an elected Welsh Assembly which would have limited legislative powers. Its members would be the buffer between Westminster and the "seat of power" in Cardiff, and the Assembly would operate outside the province of the Secretary of State for Wales and the Welsh Office. But the biggest objection to the proposal was that, although such an Assembly would give the Principality a bigger voice in Welsh claims on government, Westminster would have a supreme power of veto. Thus the Assembly would amount to little more than a toothless talking-shop, one of those councils of good intentions so beloved of the Welsh.

There was another provision which heightened opposition to what had become known as the Kilbrandon Report. If the Assembly proposal should succeed, it would mean a reduction of Welsh elected representation at Westminster by five M.P.s; and Welsh M.P.s would be entitled to the option of standing for the Assembly (every four years) instead of for their defined Westminster constituencies.

This caused an ever sharper split in the Labour Party and set alight, with even greater intensity, the arguments for and against Home Rule. The Conservatives formed a united front against any sort of devolved government. The Labour Party, however, produced a few minority groups and of these the Welsh one was the most voluble. It had only six members, but they constituted about a quarter of the Welsh Labour Group. The others were Leo Abse, Donald Anderson, Fred Evans, Ioan Evans and Ifor Davies. It was on this issue that Neil decided to make his stand, and it revealed the qualities that led to his being elected leader of his party in 1985, just twelve years later. Together with Leo Abse, M.P. for Pontypool, he directed the strategy of the anti-devolution movement for Wales and, in face of terrific odds and vicious attacks from within their own

Discussing the *first* Welsh Select Committee with its Chairman, Leo Abse, M.P..

Party, they nursed the opposition to Kilbrandon within Wales to such effect that public demand for a referendum was granted by the government. The result of that 1979 referendum in Wales was a four-to-one rejection. Even though Scotland, in its referendum, accepted the government's proposal for a Scottish Assembly, it did not have the required 40 per cent majority. The whole devolution plan was dropped for both countries and devolution taken out of the political arena for at least a decade.

With all the active preparations among the parties for an early general election inevitably the writing appeared on the wall once more. Devolution would figure among the issues, and there was no doubt early on about the embarrassment this would cause the Labour Party leader. After all, he could not disclaim a major responsibility for the scuppering of his party's efforts to grant the processes of devolved governments to Scotland and Wales in 1979. It was obvious this could be a weapon with which to berate the new leadership should the other parties be of such mind.

The Conservatives, however, decided early on not to recharge the fires of Home Rule for Wales. Welsh Secretary, Nicholas Edwards, with whom I discussed the subject early in the campaign, was content to ignore in the main, or at least play down, the issue. But with the Welsh and Scottish Nationalist parties, for whom devolution remains basic to their political ideology, again on the Home Rule rampage, it was a foregone conclusion that the ghost of 1979 would be raised for Neil Kinnock.

The Labour Party could not afford to ignore the issue and Neil was fully cognisant of the strong pro-devolution views still held by some powerful sections within the party. His dilemma was how to reconcile his previously held objections to devolution with the growing Labour demands that the party should again pronounce itself a party of devolution.

To any successful politician, however, embarrassments of policy issues are but a passing phase. His predecessor Harold

Wilson had summed it up beautifully when he declared nine days was a long time in politics—and the public memory is notoriously short-lived unless it is continually stoked up. In this particular instance it perhaps emphasised again Neil Kinnock's leadership capability that he was able to shrug off any embarrassment without entering into any new commitments. But the surprise, surely, was that the Tories, in particular, did not make more of the situation.

Nonetheless, had the result of the election been different it is still a matter of strong conjecture how the new Prime Minister would have faced up to the situation. I imagine his attitue would have been that his erstwhile personal objections were based not against the primciple of devolution but to the form of a toothless devolution embodied in the elected Assemblies which would have been subject to the supreme veto of the Westminster Parliament.

But the issue was not put to the test. I have the strongest feelings, however, that within the next quinquennial period Neil, devolutionwise at any rate, will be faced with an even more formidable situation.

His continuing leadership of the party seemed in little doubt and his objective, the key to No. 10 will remain paramount. Neil Kinnock's leadership baptism under blistering election conditions gave the Labour Party sufficient confidence to stay with him. And the spectre of Home Rule demands will not go away!

Chapter 18: Two Tragedies

The discovery of Desmond Donnelly, the ex-M.P., dead in a hotel bedroom near London Airport was the tragic climax for me of one of the longest and friendliest associations between a Lobby Correspondent and a Member of Parliament. He had taken an overdose of tablets. It was a pathetic ending to a career which, but for a bitter sell-out in the early stages of the first Wilson government in 1964, might have gone on to great things.

The Desmond Donnelly I knew so intimately was a conscientious, shrewd, able and adept politician who, during his time in Parliament as the Member for Pembroke, was true to his own principles, even though there were many times when he was in conflict with his party's policies and attitudes. He defeated Major Gwilym Lloyd George in the 1950 General Election on the promise that, if he was elected, Pembroke would get itself a good constituency M.P. It was on this promise, and not because he was standing as a Labour candidate, that he won the seat, he told me. It was at that election that I first met him when, politically, he was still under suspicion in parts of the constituency for being a convert to the Party from the ill-fated Commonwealth Party, for which earlier he had stood as a Parliamentary candidate.

What he promised, Pembroke got during his representation, which went on until 1970. He was defeated at that election, which he fought as the candidate representing the Democratic Party (which he had formed) having resigned from Labour in 1968. It was this defeat which won the seat for the Tories, for whom it has been retained ever since by Nicholas Edwards, now Secretary of State for Wales.

In the twenty years he represented Pembroke, Desmond Donnelly fought hard and persistently to put this Little England beyond Wales into the forefront of European industrial and commercial developments. It was his vision that a natural

Desmond Donnelly's last campaign.

harbour which provided the best deepwater shipping facilities in Britain's coastline should figure in the then growing oil industry, and the days of the giant oil-tankers. From this came the Conservative government's go-ahead for the development of the port and the promise by Harold Macmillan that Milford Haven would become the number two oil terminal for Europe, second only to Rotterdam.

To persuade government circles of the vast potential of his constituency as a major oil terminal, Donnelly enlisted the support (only too readily given) of the great American oil magnates. They were prepared to throw in vast sums of capital, each individual bid within the consortium outdoing the others. It was like a massive game of Poker with multi-billion-pound stakes that night when I was introduced, in secrecy and strict confidence, to the bidders.

A cryptic telephone-call one evening at the House of Commons asked me to contact Desmond Donnelly urgently. I did, and was asked to go to his flat in Gordon Mansions, a ten-minute taxi ride from Westminster. When I was admitted I found about half a dozen tycoon types and a beaming Donnelly. These were the people, I was told, whom Donnelly had gathered together to give force to his project for a Pembrokeshire oil port, and, astonishingly, I was shown figures to bear out his statement. I got as excited as anyone there, but only momentarily because, in their hearing, Donnelly explained to me that the whole project was top-secret, and emphasised by such clichés as that I had been called in to bear testimony at the right time, that the financial backing was there. I was to be given the word when the story was ready to break. I maintained silence and kept in constant touch with Donnelly, but never got the advance release. I had to take my place alongside other journalists in following up the historic announcement in the Commons by Prime Minister Macmillan of the Milford Haven oil-port development. This happened several weeks after the meeting with the oil tycoons, so by keeping quiet I lost the story of the decade, but perhaps also ensured that Milford would get the prize.

The one thing I did get out of it was that unforgettable experience in Gordon Mansions, rubbing shoulders with the Texas and other oil-magnates, and listening to them discussing multi-billion-dollar expenditures just as if they were toffee papers! It was something I could never have visualised. I gathered that the links between Donnelly and the consortium had been forged by Dean Acheson, the American Secretary of State. Since then I have got to know that he and Desmond were close and firm friends. That's the Desmond of those days! He always went for the top.

Ten years later Donnelly had taken the irretrievable step which resulted in his break with the Labour Party and the premature ending of a power-packed career. This was his bold defiance (along with fellow backbencher Woodrow Wyatt) of the 1964-65 Labour government's proposal to re-nationalise the steel industry.

On a bleak March night in 1965 the House of Commons was debating the second reading of the Enabling Bill. With a majority of only three, and the possibility of its being turned over by the two rebels unless an assurance was given that only fifty one percent of the industry would be acquired, tension was incredibly high. The government had produced a shopping-list of the large companies it proposed to take into public owner-ship again. The only way out for the government was a comp-romise.

Donnelly had kept me in constant touch with events during the day. He angrily dismissed rumours that the two of them would later receive peerages if they toed the line, but he admitted that the Chief Whip had offered a compromise if they behaved and did not wreck the Bill. Defeat on this measure could jeopardise the government's existence, dangling as it was on a very slender thread of three votes.

It was a day of high drama with no-one really knowing what the compromise would be. Harold Wilson was worried and angry because he knew, from previous experience with Donnelly, that once he had given his word that he would go through with anything, the odds against him changing his mind were considerable. And with the wily Wilson's rep-utation at that time, and the extremes to which he had been pushed to keep a rickety government intact, Donnelly reckoned he would be prepared to go a long way towards meeting the duo's demands. According to Desmond it would have to be something in the hand and not on the bush.

An hour before the 10 o'clock vote I met Donnelly in the Lobby and he warned me their revolt might not go through after all. He had received an assurance that Wilson and George Brown, who was winding up the debate, had agreed to a public declaration of a compromise which would meet their demand, or at least give some indication of a relaxation in the all-out public ownership plans. This, I recall him arguing, to me as well as to himself, would be a commitment from which the government would not be able to withdraw; and was not George Brown a personal friend for whom he, Donnelly, had stage-managed his bid for the leadership against Wilson? Even then Donnelly was uneasy, but Woodrow Wyatt signifying from the floor of the House an acceptance of this assurance, the matter seemed settled.

When George Brown rose to wind up the debate it was obvious he was under considerable stress. His speech was slurred and sluggish, and the House never heard what the actual compromise was to be. Sufficient only that the government would compromise to the extent of examining again the 51 per cent proposal . . . but there was no promise that it would endorse any proposal which was short of full nationalisation. It was on this mixed assurance that Wilson and Brown carried the division—with a surprising majority of four.

The effect on George Brown personally of this "sell-out" was demonstrated to us shortly after the debate. Those Lobby Correspondents who were following up the story suddenly received an invitation, through George Brown's Press aide, a former colleague, Bill Greig of the *Daily Mirror*, to meet him in his room in the Commons. Some of us expected an explanation of the night's events, and perhaps the text of "the compromise". We were disappointed on both counts. In his room we found a man who had been torn apart by the night's experience. I knew what was happening inside him because I had known of the strong friendship which had existed beween him and Donnelly, and how he realised, after vital votes had been won, the way in which that friend had been deceived, for deceit it was, whether wilfully on the part of George Brown, or otherwise. He sat there behind the desk showing unmistakeable signs of several drinks too many.

Between him and the drinks' hospitality cabinet in the corner of the room stood a stern-faced and resolute Sophie (Mrs., now Lady, Brown), and suggestions that drinks might be passed around met with a stony silence from that quarter. As Bill mentioned later, Sophie had been determined there would be no more drink available that night to cause any more upset than had already occurred. It was not clear why we had been summoned to his room. George had nothing to say beyond a mumbled repetition that the government would adhere to the compromise . . . which was nothing more than an assurance to consider again whether there should be a full-blooded or partial nationalisation of the industry.

In the event, as everyone expected, even, I believe, the two rebels also by that time, the government pressed on along an unchanged course. It was a shattering conclusion for Donnelly, one from which he never fully recovered. In its aftermath came the 1968 resignation from the Labour Party; his attempt in that year to form a new Commonwealth Party, for which he stood, in the Newcastle-under-Lyme by-election (suffering a massive defeat), his later efforts to win Tory support for a Conservative candidature (also rejected) and his eventual realisation that life outside practical politics was intolerable.

It was a bitterly sad sequence, one that Desmond Donnelly did not deserve, and I am glad to be able to call myself one of his friends.

A close friend of Donnelly's was Lady Megan Lloyd George. Towards the end of her thirty-five years' Parliamentary career—she was first elected as Liberal M.P. for Anglesey, which she represented from 1929 to 1951; was out of the house for six years and then became Labour M.P. for Carmarthen in 1957—I had noticed that they were almost inseparable. So had others, and the usual clutch of stories traded through the lobbies raised the question of how deeply they were involved. I can honestly say that there was nothing in any way improper about their relationship.

Eventually circumstances proved that Donnelly had become aware of something which Lady Megan kept hidden until the last few months before her death in 1966. For her last few years she had been under treatment for cancer. She had come to accept that time was running out for her, but none of her colleagues in the Labour Party was aware of it. She tried, and largely succeeded, to carry through a normal Parliamentary life. But there were times when her condition forced her to ease up, and it was then that Donnelly took on his shoulders as much of the burden of her Parliamentary responsibilities as was possible.

'Lady Megan' canvassing in the Carmarthen Constituency.

It was only natural they should become friendly from the time Lady Megan joined the Labour Party, in 1955, after having been four years in the political wilderness following her narrow defeat by Cledwyn Hughes in Anglesey in 1951. Her target as a prospective Labour Party candidate was Carmarthen, and this was the adjoining constituency to Donnelly's Pembrokeshire division. Also they were both rebels at heart.

Except for Lady Megan's burning ambition to see Home Rule for Wales, a Liberal ideal she brought into the Labour Party and shared with six other new Labour colleagues, the Donnelly-Lady Megan partnership ran smoothly. My first intimation that there was something seriously wrong with Lady Megan's health came during the run-up to the Christmas parliamentary recess in 1965. She had been away from the House for a couple of weeks. My enquiries about her whereabouts brought the reply from Criccieth, her North Wales home, that she was suffering, but recovering, from a very bad cold. She expected to be back at Westminster in the New Year.

To me that semeed to be a very long time to get over a cold. Then I heard from a source outside Parliament that Lady Megan had been a patient at the Hammersmith Hospital. I went to see Donnelly. ''Let me see what I can find out for you,'' he said, without any hint that he was well aware of what was happening. ''I'll give Megan a ring, and if she is well enough she'll probably tell you herself.'' In less than an hour he got back to me and then, over a cup of tea in the Strangers' Cafeteria, he prefaced his revelation, carefully and emphatically, with, ''David, this has got to be absolutely confidential, not a word to anyone yet, and no hints . . .''

Having received my undertaking, he told me that Megan was still at Hammersmith Hospital, that she had undergone an operation for cancer of the breast, but that she hoped shortly to go home. Under our agreement that the matter would be treated by me as strictly confidential, he went on to tell how she had been suffering from the cancer for at least a year, how he

A Dragon in the House

had assisted wherever possible with her parliamentary duties and finally made me promise not to try and contact her.

I was staggered by the whole thing. I cannot recall whether she went to North Wales for that Christmas, but early in January I received a call from Lady Olwen Carey-Evans, her sister, and another from Lady Olwen's son, Robin Carey-Evans, who was a favourite nephew of Lady Megan. Apparently they had been told by Lady Megan that I was aware of the whole story, but that I had promised not to release it yet. They were profound with their thanks and pressed me to give another assurance that the confidence would be kept. "It means so much to her and would help her to make a recovery," I was told. What was I to do? This sort of story could not be kept quiet indefinitely. Someone would be bound to hear of it. At the same time I had the horrible feeling that if I wrote it I might be responsible if Lady Megan did not make a recovery, and that once the word was out the prospective candidates for Carmarthen would start sniffing around.

I agreed with Lady Olwen to do nothing for another week, but said that I would like to speak to Lady Megan at home. I wanted to satisfy myself that at least she was able to talk and that the post-operative recovery was proceeding. It was agreed, and that evening I telephoned Criccieth. It was Donnelly who answered the telephone. He was there helping with constituency affairs and had been told to expect my call. I *did* speak to her, and she agreed I could write a piece saying she had undergone an operation before Christmas and was recuperating in North Wales. Not a word to suggest what the operation was about.

She seemed pretty cheerful as she added another piece of information regarding a constituency story. It seemed natural enough. M.P.s were always trying to get something in the papers about their constituencies. I did not see her again because, shortly after the General Election in 1964, which was fought for her in absentia by her local Management Committee and friends, particularly Gwilym Price Davies and Donnelly, Lady Megan died.

Before the General Election was declared it had become fairly public knowledge that she was seriously ill, but the fact that she had insisted on standing as the candidate for the election, which was won for her, suggested that she and the Labour Party expected a full recovery and that she would resume her seat at Westminster. Again it was Donnelly who gave me the hint that that would never be. A few days before her death I saw him in the Lobby and told him I was visiting North Wales the following week to see a friend. Would it be possible to call on Lady Megan? Again that serious look, and a promise to find out.

I was at home that weekend when Donnelly rang me from Criccieth. "Sorry," he said. "Do you mind if Megan says it isn't possible?" Her appearance had worsened so much that she did not want to meet anyone. The cancer was well into its terminal stage and she was but a shell of her old self. "But hang on," he said. A couple of minutes later a very faint voice thanked me for everything, especially for being so kind as not to write anything. Lady Megan paid her debt from her death-bed. A few days later the obituary notices were published. With my advance knowledge, mine had been prepared at least a week ahead.

This was one story I never regretted not having done; it was one of many confidences I was very glad I had honoured.

Chapter 19: Mr Speaker Thomas

The Speakership is one of the most honoured positions in the land. Until 1919 Mr. Speaker was the First Commoner, but under an Order in Council in that year he was lowered in precedence and now comes immediately after the Lord President of the Council.

It is an office which dates from 1377, and not from the first Parliament, which was assembled in 1213 after the Magna Carta. In the early days it was the most precarious of occupations, and at least nine Speakers are known to have suffered violent deaths, largely as a result of upsetting the Sovereign. Originally the Speaker was the *Sovereign's* representative in Parliament, but from the turbulent days of Charles I, when the King made his desperate and unsuccessful bid to exercise supreme control over Parliament and the Exchequer, the Speaker has been the representative of the House of Commons in its relations with the Crown.

After Charles I crashed his way into the House of Commons Chamber it was decreed by Parliament that no Sovereign would again be permitted to enter the House. This is why, even today, the State Opening of Parliament by the Monarch always takes place in the House of Lords.

Although the position of the Speaker has changed, a relic of the Charles I days still remains. Whenever the House discusses money-matters the Speaker is "moved from the Chair" and the M.P.s resolve themselves into a Committee over which the Deuputy Speaker, or the Chairman of Ways and Means, presides. The explanation of this throwback is that, as the King's man in those early days, the Speaker conveyed information about the state of the national finances to the Sovereign. When the exchequer was flush, or even when it wasn't, Royal demands would be made to boost the Royal purse for the personal upkeep of the Court or to maintain the army or whatever.

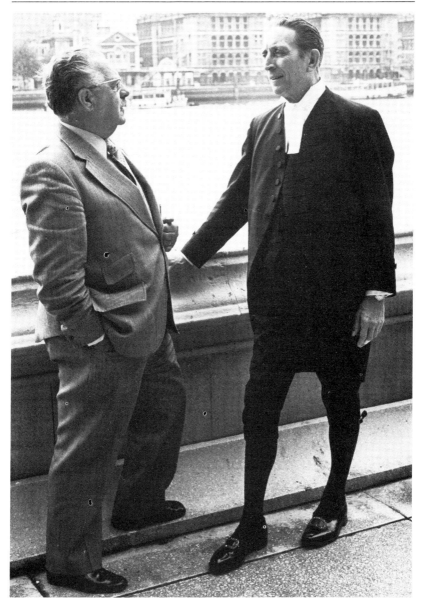

Old Friends (the Author with Mr Speaker Thomas).

There would be no question of that happening today, but tradition dies hard in Parliament and the same reason is given in the twentieth century (and no doubt will continue to be given long into the twenty-first century) as was given in the 14th Century; with the Speaker out of the way, there is no fear that secrets will be conveyed to the Sovereign.

Of all the friendships I have made during my years at Westminster, none has been more enduring and more greatly cherished than that with George. When one speaks in the House of Commons about "George", there can be only one person to whom it refers: George Thomas, formerly, and for the greater part of our forty-years' friendship, the Member for a Cardiff constituency and a pillar of the Methodist Church. He has also been Secretary of State for Wales and Speaker of the House of Commons, and is now Viscount Tonypandy. He was the one who, from the very first weeks of my sojourn at Westminster, encouraged me, helped me, and on numerous occasions was the staff on which I had to lean in making my way through the labyrinths of political and parliamentary intrigues and around the many pitfalls, as well as when enjoying the pleasanter sides of its every-day life.

Speaker Thomas will go down in the annals of that long and distinguished office as among its most respected, able, witty, human, and understanding holders. By virtue of its place and onerous responsibilities to this Mother of Parliaments, he who holds the Speakership has to be a very lonely man. He has to be above the day-to-day affairs outside the Chamber insofar as any personal, social or political involvements are concerned, if only to demonstrate that there is no preference or favouritism being shown to one side or the other. By his very nature, as a warm-hearted, Christian individual, with a generous attitude towards his fellow men and women (despite resisting the possibilities which have been open to him to surrender his bachelorhood) this aspect of the Office could well have been most oppressive and a strong factor against his continuance in it. I often wondered, at the beginning, whether George would be able to tolerate his virtual ostracism and detachment from so many on all sides of the House who were his friends and to make a success of high office.

It was to prove his measure as a man and his strength of character that not only did he take this in his stride, but he developed it to the extent that he has rightly achieved, in his own time, a fame and cherished loyalty from the House of Commons that none of his predecessors rose to. Even the greatly respected "Shakes" Morrison, who became Governor of Australia, did not quite reach the esteem and loyalty, during his short-lived period as Speaker in the mid-fifties, as has been bestowed on the Welsh-born ex-miner's son from the Valleys.

It was from "Shakes" Morrison, Scottish, stentorian of voice and rugged of countenance, deeply proud of his Gaelic up-bringing (he did speak the Gaelic, which I tried to compare with my Welsh) that I first gathered the true loneliness of Mr. Speaker. Very much like George, he was an affable character who liked the company of his fellow-parliamentarians and found pleasure and comfort within the precincts of West-minster. I got to know him pretty well and several times we met out of sitting hours, either on the Terrace or in New Palace Yard, where he liked to take a morning walk.

Unlike George, however, he was "dragooned" into the chair. George Thomas had undergone a period of "apprenticeship" as Chairman of Ways and Means and Deputy Speaker. He had, in fact, been groomed for the office which, insofar as it was within the Prime Minister's influence, had been promised him. But it was not for Harold Wilson, in this case, to instal him or ensure his succession when the time came. The choice of Speaker is the sole prerogative of the House of Commons, though no-one doubted, from the moment it was known that George would be successor to Speaker Selwyn Lloyd, that the House would unanimously endorse him.

The most striking thing about him was his call on the House to come to order. The Thomas "Order, Order" became, in no time at all, a symbol of his authority to which Members reacted with respectful acknowledgement. The Welsh lilt made it all the more attractive until, in a short while, it had become a household phrase, and its association with Mr. Speaker Thomas firmly established. These were the first words he used in an experiment for the broadcasting of the proceedings of Parliament. But there could well have been a tragic curtailment of that famous call, even before Mr. Thomas decided to stand down from the Chair . . .

Some of us had become concerned over the increasing frequency with which the Speaker's voice seemed to diminish in strength and clarity towards the end of 1977. He appeared to have what he himself explained as recurring bouts of laryngitis. It is true that at one time he had been a pretty heavy smoker, but in those days there was not the prominence given to smoking as a powerful contributory factor in lung cancer.

Not until he had suffered a mild heart-attack which kept him away from the House for some time did he decide to give up smoking cigarettes. He didn't give up smoking, however, but switched to small cigars. During his two years as Deputy Speaker these were what he smoked, and I had noticed on some occasions, when we met for a chat in the Speaker's House, that he seemed to be smoking more heavily. I always remarked upon this because he inhaled, which I thought was bad.

Before he assumed the office and full responsibilities of Speaker, and while he had more time to himself, George had often come at weekends to visit Myfanwy and me at "Four Winds". It was convenient because it was only a couple of hundred yards off the A40 roundabout in North Uxbridge, an easy run from Westminster. They were private and enjoyable visits, sometimes with friends invited for a meal.

Even when he became Speaker, he still managed the occasional visit, only these times his being driven out in Mr. Speaker's

At The Speaker's Residence, 1981.

official car meant less privacy. The local police once spotted the car being driven into my driveway and shortly afterwards I was asked about it. As an Uxbridge magistrate I used to have police officers calling at all times for signature to warrants, and it was during one of these visits that the officers casually enquired about the official car. It was suggested that in future I should notify the local police station so that a watch could be kept "just in case something went wrong". I explained that there was no need for this, since it would be a private, personal occasion, but thereafter "Four Winds" received more attention than perhaps it would otherwise have merited.

On one particular occasion, however, George had confirmed he would be coming to us on a Friday evening and Myfanwy and I had decided to invite John Griffiths and his wife, Rosemary, to meet him. This was planned because John, a close friend who had known Myfanwy since her schooldays in Llanelli, was a consultant surgeon at a well-known hospital in London, and was a foremost authority on cancer. Myfanwy and I had been very conscious of George's ''sore throats'' and thought it would do no harm to get him a private specialist opinion. I must confess that neither George nor John was aware of our purpose in bringing them together early that evening. Two other friends, Ted and Sheila Darvel, had been invited, but they were not expected until later. This would allow George and John some time together in private.

Things went according to plan. Quite cheerful and relaxed at the prospect of a friendly get-together, George, nonetheless, was showing some strain and complained about his laryngitis, though he continued to smoke his cigar. That was how it was when the Griffiths' arrived. It was their first meeting with Mr. Speaker, but there was no side or formality—we were all Welsh together. When the ladies left for the kitchen to supervise the meal, I casually suggested that John might advise George to give up smoking, since he had been complaining more about his throat recently and the House of Commons, too, had noticed an occasional croak in his ''Order, Order''.

I honestly believe George did not know there was anything seriously wrong when he agreed to open his mouth for a cursory examination; but thirty seconds later came the awful truth! John's opinion, in the privacy of that room, but with a firm professionalism which brooked no doubt, left only one question: was it too late, or would giving up smoking immediately prevent the inevitable consequences of it if he didn't?

Turning to me as he walked towards an ashtray at the far end of the room, George said simply, ''That is the last cigar I shall ever smoke.'' He was visibly shaken, but calm, as he placed the half-smoked butt into the ashtray. Quietly he thanked John and agreed to a further examination. There was no need to ask that nothing further should be said about it. He knew it was a confidence I would keep, and I reveal it now only with his permission. I have no doubt that, but for the advice he was given that evening, the strength of willpower which enabled him to give up smoking there and then, and the subsequent excellent work of his medical advisers, the House of Commons would have suffered the loss of their popular Speaker long before it happened through his voluntary decision.

That last half-butt of the offending cigar remains with us as a reminder of that providential encounter at ''Four Winds'' without which I dare not contemplate what might have happened.

In retrospect, a forty-years' friendship has gone astonishingly quickly. In that time I can recall only once when we were not ''on speaking terms''. I know it was not for long, perhaps a week or ten days, when George was on the back-benches and I was still earning my corn and learning the ways of a Lobby Correspondent. What caused it I cannot remember. Maybe I had written something of which he disapproved, or perhpas I had upset him in some other way. I do remember making it up, however. In the Lobby one evening we both decided it wasn't worth it for either of us to keep at arm's length, and whatever exaggerated sense of my own importance I may have shown as an inexperienced political journalist, I realised I needed my M.P. contacts as much as, if not more than, they needed me. From that time on, in and out of office, never was a call from one to the other ignored.

My first real recollection of George Thomas is of some weeks after I arrived at Westminster, when anxiety was being shown in the House about his disappearance during a parliamentary visit to Greece. His fellow Cardiff M.P., Jim Callaghan, had raised the matter with Foreign Secretary, Ernest Bevin, and it was thought he had been taken hostage by guerillas. I went to Cardiff that weekend and one of the sub-editors showed me a picture which was to have been carried with my story. ''He's the one on the donkey, riding back to freedom,'' I was told. I've looked everywhere for that picture without success.

Our friendship really began after this. I interviewed him about a statement in which, as a former teacher, he criticised his own government's education proposals. I had been warned he was one of the South Wales leftist rebels, but I found him anything but. He was friendly and fair. He has remained so ever since.

I learned a great deal from him about the ways of M.P.s as Lobby-fodder. I believe he will agree that I repaid him much of the debt by keeping him in the public eye whenever possible. After all, to any M.P. publicity is the stuff of success. George never betrayed a commitment to his Office or as a backbencher, and I never took unfair advantage of our friendship.

One of the first political and parliamentary campaigns in which we both figured, he as instigator and I as the witness and chronicler, was his consuming passion for a reform of the lease-hold system. This is what had featured foremost with him in his early days at Westminster because of the iniquitous effect of the "ground-landlord" system, and in South Wales particularly.

In 1960 I learned that the Parliamentary Party, made up of all the Welsh Members, was being encouraged to take up the matter at the insistence of George Thomas. Since it was constantly being raised in the House, and the Western Ground-Rents Company of Cardiff was under persistent attacks about the takeover of thousands of houses, especially in the Valleys, as hundred-year leases were expiring, I determined to follow up the story. George supplied the ammunition and unashamedly I fired it.

The Welsh Party refused to back his fight for reform, so he decided to organise a petition, and to rally public support for it by personal appearances outside the Cardiff Market on Saturdays. After he had told me his plan I went to Cardiff to see my Editor, Don Rowlands. We discussed the issue and, although he knew that, as a pro-Tory newspaper, the *Mail* would come under heavy pressure, he agreed to back George. It became the paper's social-reform campaign and it was as a result of this that signed petitions for leasehold reform poured into the Thomas campaigning-machine. Hardly a day went by that some question or other on leasehold reform did not appear on the Commons Order Paper. It took another six years, however, for the Leasehold Reform Bill of 1967 to become law. That campaign gave me a sense of satisfaction such I had never felt before, and it welded our friendship. It also gave me a greater understanding of the driving motivation which seemed to possess him whenever he set his sights on any worthwhile objective. I was not surprised when eventually he was installed as Speaker of the House of Commons.

Naturally there were times when I considered our friendship should mean special treatment. Occasionally I *was* helped, sufficiently for me to get a slight edge over my colleagues, but he never knowingly passed on information which was his only by virtue of his office as a Minister or Speaker.

Chapter 20: The Speaker speaks

Speakers do not, as a rule, allow themselves to give uninhibited interviews for publication, but when I suggested it to Mr. Speaker Thomas, shortly after he had settled into his new Office, after serious thought, he agreed. It was to be a sincere appraisal of himself in the Speakership and when it duly appeared it caused considerable interest, so much so that I consider it worthy of repetition in the present context:

"On 3rd February, 1976, the Rt. Hon. T. George Thomas, M.P. for Cardiff West, became Speaker of the House of Commons, only the second Member for a Welsh constituency ever to do so. The other was Sir John Trevor, nearly three hundred years previously.

In the tradition of the House, he was "dragged" to the Chair, an "unwilling" occupant of the Office that was once that of the King's man, but which later became its antithesis. An Office of great eminence, it imposes upon the holder a self-denial which only the strongest-willed can accept and contain. For the Speaker is a lonely figure. Not for him any more the relish of talks and companionship in those places where M.P.s congregate to gossip, speculate, and evaluate political facts and possibilities. Mr. Speaker has to remain aloof—yet friendly in a dignified way—in his disposition towards those of whose rights and privileges he is the guardian.

These Mr. Thomas can be, but for those of us who see and hear him nearly every day in session, he has retained the simple charm, benevolence, and wit which have characterised his thirty-two years as a Member of Parliament.

An observant early-morning passer-by on Westminster Bridge, which overlooks the Speaker's Residence and the House of Commons Terrace, might see, on most days, a lone figure purposefully striding along the deserted

The Two Welsh Speakers (Mr Speaker Thomas beneath the Portrait of
Mr Speaker Trevor).

Terrace. It will be the Speaker, perhaps taking the opportunity to think over the events of the day ahead, or to relax with a brief constitutional exercise before his long and demanding hours in the Chair.

As a bachelor living alone in the splendour of the Speaker's Residence, which flanks the east end of the Terrace, he is set in his ways and talks freely about them. We discussed the typical day for the Speaker. 'I am awakened at 7.30 a.m., which is as automatic as night follows day,

Morning 'Constitutional'.

however late I go to bed,' he said. 'A simple breakfast and the newspapers, a stroll on the Terrace and at nine o'clock I see my Constituency Secretary, who will be with me for threequarters of an hour. Then I see the Parliamentary Secretary, who brings all the correspondence concerning the House on the political side. Half an hour later, I see my Administrative Secretary, who brings the correspondence about the various departments in the House, and the outside engagements and invitations. After half an hour, I see my Private Secretary to discuss interviews with M.P.'s and Clerks and this lasts until 11.15 a.m., when normally some M.P. or other wants to see me. At 11.50 a.m. it is the daily conference with the Clerks of the House and the Deputy Speaker to discuss the business of the House during the day.'

M.P.'s are entitled to submit to the Speaker before noon any Private Notice Question on important matters, and this takes priority if the Speaker agrees. It is his decision. Then begins the trial of the Chamber.

At 2 p.m. there would be more interviews before the procession, which starts at 2.27 p.m. precisely. It is said that clocks and watches can be set accurately by the Speaker's tread on a particular spot en route along the Speaker's Corridor to the Chair. Can they? I asked.

'We can tell the time to the second every day,' I was told, not without a hint of pride. 'I can reach my place for prayers in the Chamber as Big Ben is striking 2.30. There has been no occasion when we have been late, and only once when we were early, which is worse than being late, because someone was locked out of prayers.'

What thoughts pass through the Speaker's mind as, day after day, he does the same measured three-minutes' walk? Is he oblivious of the crowded lobbies and the lines of Strangers?

'Oblivious? I look straight ahead because it spoils the dignity of the procession to acknowledge people on both sides. I am conscious of M.P.'s bowing as Mr. Speaker (*not* George Thomas) passes, but I very rarely see who they are, because I am looking to the front. I only see movements out of the corner of my eye. I think this procession does something for the dignity of Parliament, and dignity and authority are very closely linked in my mind.'

Prayers over, there comes the most demanding time of the day, Question Hour. 'It is never easy to decide when enough questions have been asked on one issue and to move on to the next,' Mr. Speaker confessed. 'But experience gives one the feel for realising or thinking the time has come to move on to the next question.'

Come 5 o'clock, the Speaker leaves the Chair, often unnoticed, for a cup of tea in his private room. Some visitors may share the teatime, but then it is time for more inverviewing, and to go over papers submitted by the Clerk before returning to the Chair at 6.30 p.m. At 7.30 it is dinner-time, and two hours later the Speaker returns to the Chair until 11 p.m. or the end of the sitting.

Is it a tedious and all-demanding existence? To this Mr. Speaker Thomas's reply was, 'I think everyone should count their blessings if they have a job that is demanding and rewarding at the same time. It is not the hours that is the strain for the Speaker. It is the tension that can come in certain periods. There are occasions when the House will be feeling deeply about the question of the conduct of some of its Members, when I know before I go into the Chamber I can expect tension there. A man would be a stone if he was not affected by this feeling, and whatever I am, I am no stone. No Welshman can be without reaction to the emotions of others. But the Speaker has, before all things, to avoid feeling so involved that his emotions also are disturbed. It is vital for the House that the Speaker keeps a cool head whatever passions are raging in the Chamber.'

Is the position really a lonely one? I ventured. 'It *is* a very lonely job,' he admitted. 'It is the loneliest of jobs. Although I am of the House I have to remain apart from the House; not visiting the Members' Dining-Room, Smoke-Room, Tea-Room or Library, where M.P.'s gather. I have been given a splendid house and am expected to stay in it. Of course, I get so many M.P.'s to see me that I defeat the loneliness, by and large. And sometimes I wonder when I am going to have a minute to myself after thirty-two years! I have most missed the fellowship of the Members' Tea-Room and sitting around the Welsh table with the boys, discussing issues and people. We Welsh people like talking about people. I also miss the freedom to give my own opinions, because I now have to listen to other people's opinions instead of expressing my own.'

Rather ruefully, and somewhat disconsolate, I thought, he went on: 'I am now outside the battle, however. I am also outside party politics and not above it. The very fibre of our democratic system is the clash of party opinion. We owe all our progress to that. I am always deeply conscious that the House of Commons is still the custodian of the rights of our people's freedom of speech, worship, equality before the law and the other freedoms which we take for granted but which only exist so long as we have the House of Commons. If this place were undermined our freedom would disappear overnight. Within the House, therefore, I have special responsibility to ensure that unpopular cases get the chance to be heard. I am the protector of back-benchers' rights, and even the parties' sometimes.'

On the question of Parliamentary Privilege being the necessary instrument of our democracy it has been claimed to be, the Speaker observed: 'I regard it as a major part of my duty to protect the privilege of M.P.'s to say things in this House that cannot be said outside. This is in the interest of the community as a whole, but I try to see that if personal attacks are made on individuals outside the House, then they are at least done in Parliamentary language. But the House must be free to say things here without fear of arrest or legal action. This is a vital part of the maintenance of freedom over the rest of the country.'

What, I wondered, were the most memorable occasions since he became Speaker? There was no hesitation. 'One of the most exciting was the night I had to suspend the sitting. One group was singing "The Red Flag". A Member (it was the Rt. Hon. Michael Heseltine, Mrs. Thatcher's Minister of Defence) seized the Mace. The more this House changes the more it stays the same' (he mused paradoxically). 'We have always had our characters. We have them today. When the House ceases to have colourful characters it will cease to be the House of Commons. But it is a much more orderly House than in Gladstone's time, when M.P.s crowed like cockerels and brayed like donkeys to drown out people they did not want to hear. This House is very conscious that it is the senior parliament among the democracies of the world. We have had telephone-calls from Australian and Canadian Parliaments seeking advice on procedure. They base their systems on this House and I know from other Speakers in the Commonwealth that they all read Hansard, and that rulings we make are copied in the Commonwealth.'

The problems of the Speakership are great and many, but one in particular was recalled by Mr. Thomas. 'I went through agonies about Maxwell-Hyslop's point-of-order on the hybridity of the Shipbuilding Bill, he recalled. 'It was not easy for me, in my first few weeks, to have to give a ruling that would create havoc to the government's legislative and economic programme, but my duty is to the House not the Executive. In the event I was supported by the examiners of the Bill, but it is not easy when you have a complicated point out of the blue. If I am flummoxed I ask the House for time to give the ruling tomorrow. The House is very fair because it knows it is dangerous for Mr. Speaker to give major rulings off the cuff. Though the Clerks proffer their advice the decision must be the Speaker's.'

Do issues that were personal involvements present difficulties? Promptly came the reply, 'It is hard to believe but absolutely true, that having decided I am out of the party-political battle I never allow myself to feel involved in the great arguments going on around me. In the old days I would have taken a prominent part but I know the House has asked me to do a special job and I leave those issues without any heartburn to those still in them. I am never tempted to speak.'

On the fascinating subject of traditions in Parliament, the Speaker agrees they are basic to the continuance and fulfilment of the House of Commons. 'I regard the traditions of the House as sacred trusts. They have been built up over the centuries. Nonetheless there is one I consciously decided to bring to an end. On the rare occasion when a Speaker is called upon to reprimand a Member, I will never put that Black Hat on my head. It was last done in Mr. Speaker King's time when Tam Dalyell was reprimanded. I believed it to be an unnecessary and cruel ritual which we could well do without in this age. The reprimand itself is enough of a trial for the person concerned without the charade of the Black Hat as if he was being sentenced to death.'

With his Welsh lilt and his ready wit Mr. Speaker Thomas has built up a reputation of being the most popular and respected of contemporary Speakers. He delights in stories against himself, such as, 'Once I was fortunate. A Liverpool M.P., Mr. Eddie Loydon, was

Mr Speaker socialising with the Author, Mr. David Cole
and Mr David Thomas.

speaking to a crowded House when Mrs. Winifred Ewing, a
Scottish Member, called in a loud voice that she could not
understand a word the Honourable Member was saying.
Naturally enough Mr. Loydon, far from looking pleased,
was very angry. There were shouts from the Chamber but
when I said, ''Order, Order, there are many accents in this
House. I only wish I had one myself,'' the House responded
with a laugh. Even Eddie Loydon laughed and it passed
over. My feeling is that if one is fortunate enough to be able
to defuse high feelings by a light word at one's own
expense it is the best way of doing it.'

Later, in its tribute to Mr. Speaker Thomas, the *House
Magazine* stated: ''A Welshman with the music of Wales
in his voice, full of charm and totally lacking pomposity
whilst remaining a dignified occupant of the Chair. A
popular respected figure . . .''

I have found no-one who could disagree with this testimony
to the man, even though he did, in *Mr. Speaker*, his autobiography, find a handful of critics over his upbraiding of some
former colleagues and their association with certain events.

Chapter 21: Decline and Fall

Where are the Churchills, the Bevans, the Lloyd Georges, the Stanleys and the Macmillans of today? Since Michael Foot retreated into the shadows, and Enoch Powell's controversial forays have become more occasional and more predictable, the House of Commons is suffering increasingly from a dearth of orators. It is a lamentable fact.

I always admired Michael's charisma at the Despatch Box, his rapid change of tone and inflection and his extensive abrasive or mollifying tactics according to the issue and mood of the House. I shall always admire his capacity and courage in embarking on major speeches without a prepared script, and apparently not a single reference except where the rules of the House demand that certain papers and statistics are laid on the Table.

But I nearly always despaired of taking a verbatim of his speeches because he *would* fail to reach a conclusion in his sentences. Nearly always he struck out on a new tack which left one hanging in mid-air. His delivery, however, was so artistic that the listener would hardly detect this. As an orator (though his critics often likened him more to the mob tub-thumper) he is indubitably the last of the post-war breed. He could pack the House no matter what the debate was about. But his greatest effect was as the Prosecuting Attorney. He would flay his opponents unmercifully, while, when he was required to be constructive in the sense of advocating alternatives to those issues which he was attacking, he seldom seemed to have the power to rouse his audience to the same pitch. On the whole, and maybe it is because of the perpetuality of our national crises and Party problems, speeches in the House nowadays tend to be more in the Party sledgehammer mould, and lacking in the finesse and polish which was practised by the old-style orators and which delighted their listeners.

One whom I would have dearly loved to have heard in his hey-day was the 'Welsh Wizard', David Lloyd George, but he died some months before I arrived at Westminster. It was said of him that in full flow he could charm the nightingales off the trees along the banks of the Severn. I do not know in what connection this was said of him, whether there were any *special* nightingales along the banks of the river which separates Wales from England or whether it was a comment on one of his famous speeches which was delivered at Newnham, on the banks of the Severn.

I have been fortunate enough, however, to have heard and reported all those who made their mark on the parliamentary and political scenes since the war. Foremost, of course, was Winston Churchill. When he stood at the Despatch Box, whether as Prime Minister, Leader of the Opposition, or, later, as Father of the House from the traditional seat on the front bench below the gangway, he would be assured of a maximum audience. It was not only what he had to say but the manner in which it was delivered which formed the attraction. He was in every sense a parliamentarian for every occasion, not even above a little gamesmanship to put off his opposite number in the House on big occasions. I can recall one particular incident vividly and the subterfuge he adopted when Prime Minister Attlee was addressing the House in an opening speech on the India Bill. It was a really major occasion and the House was hanging on to every word. Attlee had been on his feet for about a quarter of an hour when there was a slight commotion on the Opposition Front Bench.

Clem paused and looked over his spectacles at Winston, who was fumbling in an agitated manner and, with head bent, conveyed to a packed House that something was wrong. Not a word was said. The silence was tremendous and lasted for what seemed an age. The Prime Minister, arms resting on the Despatch Box, had a quizzical look, but said nothing. Suddenly Churchill looked up and across the table, the object of everyone's gaze. He put on his most cherubic grin, muttered something inaudible and waved the Prime Minister to carry on. It came as a vast relief and the entire House dissolved with laughter. All, that is, except poor Clem. He tried hard to take up the reins again, but the moment had gone. He had lost the House. What followed was little more than the reading of a carefully prepared script in which M.P.'s seemed to have little interest. It was a Churchill ploy, of course. It was no accident, just one of those tricks which an experienced parliamentarian would resort to in order to break a speaker's hold on the House.

Another trick is to interrupt someone on their feet by raising a spurious Point of Order, but Mr. Speaker is very firm about this type of interjection and guilty M.P.'s get a real wigging, and a black mark in the Speaker's "book". Yet another Churchill incident occurred some while later when he apparently lost his "ju-jube", a little sweet he used to suck. This time Hugh Gaitskell was at the receiving end during a major economic debate, and the tactic was equally effective. In this way Winston got around one of the strict rules of the House, which forbids two Members being on their feet simultaneously if it is the intention to interrupt the one who has the Floor. And it is far more effective—just as he got around the unparliamentary expression rule by calling a lie a "terminological inexactitude".

I prefer to think of those first twenty years after 1945 as the Period of the Giants. On reflection that may be because, in the manner of the conduct of parliamentary affairs in that period, more was seen of the party leaders and their teams in the day-to-day management of the nation's affairs. Ministers and their opposite numbers had to stand up in Parliament and defend their policies and actions in full public gaze. The civil servants were less in evidence than today. They were, indeed, the faceless ones in the side wings. It was the boss who took the heat at the Despatch Box.

The changes in this respect have been much highlighted in the Falklands and Westlands affairs in which senior civil servants were featured publicly. No more the faceless wonders! Parliamentary debates, too, were more about the wider issues than what Harold Macmillan once described as ''little local difficulties'' when his government was about to topple. Britain had a much bigger stake in international affairs, and the Commonwealth was growing up to replace the Empire. M.P.'s figured more in foreign affairs and defence debates, to which several sessions were devoted. The Common Market was still something for the future and did not figure (except for its fore-runner, the Benelux Community) and the Schumann Plan for iron, coal and steel occupied a great deal of attention.

There were debates on the economy, housing, unemployment, local government reforms and so on, of course. These were the forums during which government proposals were formally and thoroughly aired, and many a parliamentary reputation was made in the course of them. Ian MacLeod's emergence during a debate on the health service, when he cast aside his prepared backbench speech and waded into Nye Bevan, its architect, was one example. It was much more open work then and M.P.s preferred to conduct their affairs on the Floor of the House; all stages of Bills were more likely to be given consideration in public rather than Standing Committees.

Then came the pressures of increasing legislation which has turned both Houses of Parliament into legislative sausage-machines, able to function only by delegating business to committees. I say that this delegation has removed much of the work of Parliament from open public gaze because, although the public are not excluded from Committees when in session, few people are aware of this or take the trouble to attend. In any case, the facilities for public attendance are very sparse. The increased work-load of M.P.'s since the 'seventies, arising from Britain's membership of the Common Market, has meant a proliferation of committees, including Select Committees, and this system of devolved responsibilities in so many different areas is anything but an aid to open government.

Another change which has become more apparent in the last five years is the place of the House of Lords in both the legislative and general operations of Westminster. Their Lordships have become more involved in legislative processes and one result is that the House of Lords, for centuries the restraining influence on the Lower Chamber, is acutely more Party politically conscious and involved. In the nature of our unwritten Constitution, the House of Lords has always had its rightful part to play in law-making. Nothing reaches the Statute Book without passage through the Upper House. But nowadays the whole tenor of The Other Place seems to be centred on Party motivations. It has become a reflection of the elected House in thought and in manner.

Gone, it seems, are the days when, if one wanted to hear expert opinions on any issues expressed in general debates, one went for a couple of hours to the tranquillity and authority of the House of Lords. Then it was the norm that, except for a few politically-minded individuals, only those who had expert knowledge of the particular subject under debate would deign to speak, and what they said was heeded. With the proliferation of Life Peerages, earned mainly on the combat-field of the House of Commons or as an acknowledgement of party political services, the House of Lords' debates generally follow the House of Commons pattern of scoring as many Party points as possible. There is little pleasure now for the likes of me in visiting their Lordships' place to get away from the scrummages, the hurly-burly and party-baiting of the Commons. Only the names, not the faces or the manners, are different. Regrettably, in my view, it has become virtually a carbon-copy and, as such, is playing very much into the hands of the militants who have been campaigning for the abolition of the second, unelected Chamber.

Forty years at the Seat of Government, stalking the corridors of Westminster, have been a long stint. I have had experiences and become involved in situations which I could never have

'The Final Edition' (the Author with John Giddings and Don Rowlands—former editors—Duncan Gardiner, John Gay Davies and a visiting American Journalist).

Retirement Dinner, Cardiff, 1981.

Speaker's Special Retirement Reception (an historical precedent) for the
Author; 1981, at The Speaker's Residence.

dreamed of in my younger days. One of my happiest days at
Westminster was when, having received the M.B.E. in the
Honours List for 1970/71, for "services to the Principality",
and with the full backing (as I was assured by the then Secretary
of State, Peter Thomas, Q.C. and his Minister of State, David
(now Lord) Gibson Watt of the Welsh Office), Myfanwy, my
sons, David and Nigel, and my daughter, Marilyn, attended my
investiture at Buckingham Palace. I also count high among my
good fortune the recognition, granted to me before my retirement from full-time parliamentary reporting, of inclusion in
the Gorsedd of Bards, with the title Dafydd ap Elli.

I shall always treasure my experiences and be happy to share
them with others. I still do not want to go from Westminster,

and thanks to the kindness of the newspaper I have served for nigh on fifty years, my term is not yet quite over. My accreditation continues until 1989. God has been good to me and to those of my family who have sustained me through the long years of irregular and protracted hours. I hope that I may even be vouchsafed a second breath with which to record yet more of those events and incidents which, from the powerful action of nostalgia upon a still-active mind, keep flooding back.

At Buckingham Palace for MBE Investiture.
Nigel, Marilyn, David G., Myfanwy and David Rosser
June 1974

'For Services to the Principality'—David Rosser, M.B.E., J.P. and
Mrs. Myfanwy Rosser at the Buckingham Palace Investiture, 1974.